A GUIDE TO
WELSH PLACE-NAMES

For my Mother
and Father

A Guide To
Welsh Place-Names

by
Anthony Lias

No. 3
WELSH HERITAGE SERIES

First published in 1994
by Gwasg Carreg Gwalch,
12 Iard yr Orsaf, Llanrwst, Wales LL26 0EH
☎ 01492 642031   📠 01492 641502

Printed and published in Wales

Contents

Preface

There are probably many people in both Wales and England who would like to know more about Welsh place-names but who have little or no knowledge of the Welsh language. This is exactly the situation in which the author found himself on coming to live in the Borderlands more than 20 years ago; and it was then — the scarcity of easily-accessible work on the subject having made a deep impression — that the seeds of the present book were sown.

Its purpose is really threefold. The first and most obvious aim has been to give the meanings of as many names in Wales itself as seemed suitable to the overall scheme; in the event these number around 500. However, for the benefit of anyone who (again like the author) is inquisitive about such matters, explanations have been put forward regarding the actual construction of Welsh names; it is hoped that the introduction here of simple symbols may prove to be of value.

Secondly, there is some discussion of the position occupied by place-names in our general consciousness. This is a theme which, although little explored hitherto, is nevertheless just as valid in Wales as it is in England — indeed, within certain limits prescribed by language, parallels can be drawn between the attitudes adopted towards 'location markers' in each of the two countries. Thirdly and lastly, consideration is given to the ways in which the Anglo-Saxon settlers of Lowland Britain adapted Brythonic names to the needs of their own (Old English) tongue. This topic, it was felt, makes for a fitting conclusion not only because it has interest for readers on both sides of Offa's Dyke, but also because it can be grasped more easily in the light of various points made in earlier chapters.

For the modern forms of Welsh place names used throughout the book, recourse has been made almost exclusively to *Rhestr o Enwau Lleoedd: A Gazetteer of Welsh Place-names*, edited by Elwyn Davies, 2nd edition (Cardiff, 1957) and/or to *Welsh Administrative and Territorial Units*, by Melville Richards (Cardiff, 1969); but, it should be noted, a departure is made from these works in that the places are referred uniformly to the Welsh counties relevant at the time of writing in 1993, viz. Clwyd, Dyfed, Glamorgan, Gwent, Gwynedd, Powys. For reasons of convenience, too, English county names and their abbreviations follow the usage in Eilert Ekwall's *Dictionary of English Place-Names*, 4th edition (Oxford, 1960).

The dates assigned in Chapter 1 to the beginnings of significant Anglo-Saxon activity in Britain are based chiefly on the arguments of J.R. Morris in *The Age of Arthur* (London, 1973).

Finally, the author must bear responsibility for any errors of fact in the pages that follow; as regards opinions, he sincerely hopes that those of other writers on the subject(s) under discussion have nowhere been misrepresented.

Abbreviations

The abbreviations used throughout the text for the counties of Wales and England are as follows, in alphabetical order (note that Môn, i.e. Anglesey, is not abbreviated):

Bd	Bedfordshire	Le	Leicestershire
Bk	Buckinghamshire	Li	Lincolnshire
Brk	Berkshire		
Ca	Cambridgeshire	Mx	Middlesex
Chs	Cheshire	Nb	Northumberland
Clw	Clwyd	Nf	Norfolk
Co	Cornwall	Np	Northamptonshire
Cu	Cumberland	Nt	Nottinghamshire
D	Devonshire	O	Oxfordshire
Db	Derbyshire	Pow	Powys
Do	Dorset	Ru	Rutland
Du	Durham	Sa	Salop
Dyf	Dyfed	Sf	Suffolk
Ess	Essex	So	Somerset
Gl	Gloucestershire	Sr	Surrey
Gla	Glamorgan	St	Staffordshire
Gw	Gwent	Sx	Sussex
Gwy	Gwynedd	W	Wiltshire
Ha	Hampshire	Wa	Warwickshire
He	Herefordshire	We	Westmoreland
Hrt	Hertfordshire	Wo	Worcestershire
Hu	Huntingdonshire	YE	Yorkshire (East Riding)
K	Kent	YN	Yorkshire (North Riding)
La	Lancashire	YW	Yorkshire (West Riding)

Introduction

Since most of what follows is devoted to the place-names of Wales as they appear in their present-day forms, it will be helpful and indeed necessary to say something about those basic mechanisms of the Welsh language which are more or less uniformly represented in the place-names themselves.

It seems better to deal with this question at the very outset than to delay it until some subsequent stage. The question is not so very difficult once one comes to grips with it; and if it is disposed of here, the reader is provided with a fixed reference point to which he or she can return at will. In practice, it will be found that the more one looks at the place-names, the less and less troublesome do the language-mechanisms become.

Lenition

By far the most important feature to bear in mind is *lenition*.

As part of a series of complex phonological changes which took place in Late Brythonic (c. 450-550, see Chapter 1), the consonants *b, c, d, g, m, p* and *t* in the interior of words were softened to *v, g, th* (voiced), *y, v, b* and *d* respectively when they occurred between vowels or between vowels and sonants (the representation of the lenited sound here is only approximately accurate, but it will serve to illustrate the general point). This is known as 'soft mutation', or 'lenition'; and an example of it is provided by the personal name *Cunotamos, which became *Cuno*dav*(os) eventually resulting (with loss of medial -*o*- and final -*os*) in Welsh Cyndaf.

Interior lenitions have long since — so to speak — melded into the fabric of Welsh speech, and are naturally no longer perceived as changes. The related phenomenon with which we are mostly concerned in place-names involves lenition of *initial* consonants under certain conditions as described below. Meanwhile here is a table of the consonant-changes themselves:

b-	→	f-
c-	→	g-
d-	→	dd-
g-	→	-
ll-	→	l-
m-	→	f-
p-	→	b-
rh-	→	r-
t-	→	d-

(Welsh *f-*, *-f* are pronounced like English *v-* in *veal* and English *-f* in *of*.)

When Does Lenition Occur?

With the reminder that nouns in Welsh are either masculine or feminine in gender, the changes just set out occur as follows (actual place-names have been used as examples, but it should be noted that exceptions are found among place-names as a whole):

(a) In feminine singular nouns when preceded by the definite article *y*, *yr*, *'r*: *caer*, 'fort', but **Y Gaer** (Gla, Pow), 'The fort'; *gorsedd*, 'tumulus', but **Yr Orsedd** (Clw), 'The tumulus'; *dôl*, 'meadow', but **Tre'r-ddôl** (Dyf), 'Hamlet (of) the meadow'.

Neither *ll-* nor *rh-* is normally affected under this heading. So, perhaps, **Y Rhiw** (Gwy), 'The slope' — though *rhiw* is sometimes treated as masculine.

(b) In adjectives following feminine singular nouns: *esgair*, 'ridge', *du*, 'black', but **Esgair Ddu** (Pow), 'Ridge black'; *carreg*, 'stone', *gwen*, 'white', but **Carreg Wen** (Pow), 'Stone white'.

Note that *gwen* is the feminine form of *gwyn*, which can mean 'fair' as well as 'white'. Some other Welsh adjectives have distinctive feminines, and these will be pointed out as they occur.

(c) In nouns of either gender when adjectives precede them: *hir*, 'long', *mynydd* (masculine), 'mountain', but **Hirfynydd** (Gla), 'Long-mountain'; *dŵr* (feminine), 'water', but **Gwenddwr** (Pow),

10

'White-water', 'Fair-water'; *hen*, 'old', *castell* (masculine), 'castle', but **Hen Gastell** (Pow), 'Old castle'.

Only a few adjectives in Welsh usually precede nouns as a matter of course; *hen* is one of these.

(d) In nouns of either gender when preceded by qualifying nouns: *maen*, 'stone', *tŷ*, 'house', but **Maendy** (Gla), 'Stone house'; *moch*, 'pigs', 'swine', *tre*, 'hamlet', but **Mochdre** (Clw, Pow), literally 'Swine hamlet'.

(e) In qualifying nouns when preceded by a feminine singular noun: *coed* (masculine), 'wood', but **Tre-goed** (Pow), 'Hamlet (of) wood'; *croes* (feminine), 'cross', but **Tre-groes** (Dyf), 'Hamlet (of) cross'.

(f) In masculine nouns when preceded by the numeral *dau*, 'two', and in feminine nouns when preceded by *dwy* (feminine form of *dau*).

(g) In nouns of either gender after certain prepositions.

It will be noticed that, in all the place-name examples given so far, the *Welsh* word-order has been followed in translation; thus Esgair Ddu, 'Ridge black' — *not* 'Black ridge', as one would normally say in English. This practice will be adhered to throughout the book, since it helps to avoid confusions. English word-order will be used only when the Welsh order coincides with it — as with Hen Gastell, 'Old castle'.

Finally — it is obvious that for a place-name like Tre-groes, in (e) above, 'Hamlet (with) cross' or 'Hamlet (at) cross' might be just as good a rendering as 'Hamlet (of) cross'. For the sake of consistency, however, and because no real violence is done to meanings, '(of)' will be used as the linking preposition in all names of this particular type.

Chapter 1

The General Background

At the time of the Roman invasion in 43 AD, most of our island was inhabited by a people of Celtic stock who called themselves *Brittones*, 'Britons', 'Brythons' (Welsh *Brythoniaid*), their language *Brittonicā*, 'Brythonic' (Welsh *Brythoneg*), and their country *Britannia*, 'Britain' (Welsh *Prydain*, from earlier *Pritannia* or *Pretannia*).

The Brythonic language was, like Gaulish, descended from the *P*- branch of Common Celtic; from the related *Q*- branch came Goidelic, ancestor of Irish Gaelic, Scottish Gaelic, and Manx. (In the latter branch the sound q^w was preserved, in the former it changed to p, hence the terminology.)

Mainland Britain beyond Forth and Clyde was dominated by the *Caledonii* (later known as Picts), a somewhat mysterious people whose language — possibly of non-Indo-European origin — is thought to have been subsequently influenced by Brythonic. The region now referred to as *Wales* in English and as *Cymru* in Welsh was occupied by four tribes whose names were recorded by the Romans as *Ordovices*, *Deceangli*, *Demetae* and *Silures* — the territories of the first two answering roughly to modern Gwynedd, those of the other two to Dyfed and Glamorgan/Gwent respectively. (A fifth tribe, the *Cornovii*, may have held parts of what is now Powys.)

Not a great deal can be said with certainty about the part played by Brythonic speech in the Roman scheme of things up to the departure of the legions, c. 410. Obviously, however, it survived and continued to develop, in the process absorbing a fair number of Latin words which shared in the development. (Many Britons — notable examples being the controversial Pelagius and, at the other end of the scale, St Patrick — learned to speak and write Latin as a necessary accomplishment.) As regards the place-names of Britain, the Roman administrators recorded a significant number for their own purposes; these names, which have come down to us from a variety of sources and about which something will be said in Chapter 6, go under the generic description *Romano-British*.

The Romans were also well acquainted with the people who, in due course, were to change the make-up of lowland Britain for ever. Raids by Saxon pirates along Britain's coasts had begun as early as the 3rd century, necessitating the creation of 'Saxon Shore' forts such as those at Reculver (Romano-British *Regulbium*) in Kent and Burgh Castle (*Gariannum*) in Suffolk, among others. Indeed, it seems not impossible that by the first half of the 5th century — when the British king Vortigern sought Saxon help against the Irish and the Picts — these seafarers had gained some degree of familiarity with certain coastal and riverine areas of the island; perhaps, too, they knew something of its place-names.

Allies and Rebels

The exact sequence of events between the first quarter of the 5th century and the second half of the 6th is by no means clear. However, it would appear that Vortigern originally stationed a number of Saxons (from now on the term 'Anglo-Saxons' will be used to embrace Angles, Saxons, Jutes and Frisians) in various parts of eastern England with the status of federates; this may have been as early as the 420s. Subsequently, against a blurred background of intrigues and shifting alliances, the federates seem to have staged two separate rebellions against their British paymasters.

The second rebellion, beginning around 460, was followed by a protracted war, which ended at some time in the 490s with a British victory at Badon (site still unidentified). It was during this lengthy struggle that Ambrosius, and after him the renowned Arthur, performed their stirring feats on the British side. The next half-century saw the Anglo-Saxons unable, or unwilling, to extend such territorial gains as they had made.

However, the state of Britain had greatly declined as a result of years of fighting, causing thousands of Britons to flee across the

Channel into western Armorica — now Brittany, whose Breton name, *Breizh*, is descended from **Brittia*, a 6th-century form originally denoting Britain itself. The Breton language is essentially Brythonic, and many similarities exist between Breton place-names and those of Wales and Cornwall.

English and Welsh

The peace brought about by the British victory at Badon was shattered in the 570s. Now began a series of renewed Anglo-Saxon assaults which, lasting on and off for more than 150 years, drove the Britons steadily westwards until most of lowland Britain had passed irrevocably out of their control.

The Anglo-Saxons, of course, were a Germanic people whose language — now usually referred to as Old English — was closely related to the Old Norse spoken by the Vikings who came later. In Anglo-Saxon eyes the British were a foreign people — a view reflected in the Old English term *walas*, 'foreigners', used to describe them. (A fuller term was *Bryt-walas*, the *Bryt-* echoing the **Brittones* mentioned in the first paragraph.) More specifically, *walas* seems to have denoted 'foreigners' who had been influenced by Roman culture and language.

This *walas* led directly to the English designation **Wales**. The adjective, *Welsh*, stems from Old English *Welisc*. One can therefore appreciate the wry humour with which Bedwyr Lewis Jones, in his book *Enwau* ('Names'), tells his Welsh readers: '*Estron oeddem ni . . . , hyd yn oed yn ein gwlad ein hunain!*' ('We were foreign . . . , even in our own country!') For it is easy to forget that nearly all Britain was once, indeed, 'Welsh'.

The word *Cymry*, now denoting the inhabitants of **Cymru** (Wales), is descended from Brythonic **Combrogī*, 'Fellow-countrymen'. The same word provided the first element of the name **Cumberland** (Old English *Cumbra-land*), originally denoting an area which extended from the Clyde to the Ribble and included the British kingdom of Rheged; the Cymry of Wales were cut off from this area by the British defeat in the battle of Chester (c. 616).

Cornwall derives from Old English *Corn-walas*, which itself consists of the base of Brythonic **Cornowiā* (Welsh *Cernyw*) with *walas* added; the meaning is probably 'Foreigners of the horn (of land)'. The *Anglo-Saxon Chronicle* also refers to the Cornwall-British as *West-Walas*, 'West Welsh', apparently in order to distinguish them from the *North-Walas*, 'North Welsh', of Wales. Cornwall, Devon and parts of Somerset belonged to the *Dumnonii* — this name being at the root of both the English **Devon** and its Welsh equivalent, **Dyfnaint**. The area had been cut off from its northern neighbours by the earlier defeat at Dyrham, near Bath, in 577.

Language Periods

A brief note on the different periods into which the history of Welsh is divided may prove useful — particularly in the context of Chapter 6, which discusses some of the ways in which the Anglo-Saxons took over place-names of Celtic provenance in what is now England.

The first 100 years or so of Anglo-Saxon activity in Britain falls within the period of *Late Brythonic*; by the end of this period, c. 550, Welsh, Breton and Cornish had already begun to go their separate ways. Most of the native place-names taken over by the Anglo-Saxons during their advance westwards had continued their development into the stage of *Primitive Welsh*, c. 550-c. 775 — the end of this stage roughly coinciding with the building of Offa's Dyke.

Old Welsh, c. 775-c. 1135, saw the emergence of written records — though some of these must have drawn heavily on older traditions. *Middle Welsh* continued down to the 14th century, and for the language subsequently *Modern Welsh* is used. Welsh people today, of course, refer to their spoken tongue as *Cymraeg* — which, in turn, derives from Brythonic **Combrogicā*, echoing the **Combrogī*. 'Fellow-countrymen', noted above.

A considerable number of place-names still extant in Wales appear in the *Liber Landavensis* ('Book of Llandaff'), a collection of charters and other records compiled c. 1135 in connection with the church at Llandaff. As compared with the state of affairs in England, comparatively few names were recorded before this date, and still fewer can boast Romano-British forms. Nevertheless, there is no reason to doubt that Welsh place-names are often very old — in certain cases pre-dating the arrival of the Romans themselves.

(Note: In Old Welsh spelling, lenition is not usually represented. Thus in the *Book of Llandaff* Caerfyrddin is spelt *Cair Mirdin*, showing neither *M*- nor -*d*- lenited; but the name will have been *pronounced* as it is today.)

Chapter 2

Ways of Constructing Place-Names in Welsh

In general it seems true to say that, for speakers of Welsh, the place-names of their native country present far fewer problems as regards meaning than do their counterparts in England for ordinary English people, and some of the possible reasons for this will be discussed in a later chapter.

Nevertheless, Wales is not without its share of names whose forms as written or spoken today represent deviations from older and more correct versions, as the following examples serve to show.

Aberhonddu (Pow) signifies 'Confluence of (river) Honddu' (with the Wye). However, *Honddu* itself is devoid of meaning as it stands — being a corruption of an older *Hoddni*, which contains the word *hawdd*, 'pleasant'. This same *Hoddni* (or *Hodni*) is behind the name **Llanthony** (Gw), standing for *Nant Hodni* — where, by association with *llan*, the first element *nant*, 'stream' has become *Llant-* (a not uncommon happening).

In the *Book of Llandaff*, the name of the river on which stands the present **Abergavenny** (Gw) is written *Geuenni* (i.e. *Gevenni*), this form stemming from Brythonic **Gobanniā*, 'Blacksmiths' river'. In this instance the initial *Ge-* appears to have become confused with the Welsh definite article, *y* — and the resulting **Y Fenni** is of course still found, denoting Abergavenny itself. The latter name means 'Confluence of (river) Gavenny' (with the Usk); but it is worth noting how far the Y Fenni variant has departed from the original Brythonic river-name.

The conjuring of a 'phantom' definite article plays a part in other corruptions, too. **Aberffraw** (Môn) was earlier *Aberffrawf*, with *-f* from original *-m-* (an example of interior lenition); this final *-f* was lost, and the resulting Aberffraw, or rather *Aberffro*, gave rise to the colloquial form *Y Berffro*. In this case — as in the next — the main reason was the shifting of the stress (accent) onto the *-e-* of

Aber; this caused initial *A-* to be heard as *Y*. Aberffraw itself signifies 'Mouth of (river) Ffraw' (probably 'Spilling river', 'Flood').

The earlier and correct form of **Abermo** (Gwy) was *Abermawdd*, 'Mouth of (river) Mawdd' — this second element being perhaps the relic of a personal name. Here again, the stress shifted from *Mawdd* (where it had rested through the Primitive Welsh period and beyond) to the *-e-* of *Aber-*, the whole name being treated as a single word; this led in due course to the corrupt form *Y Bermo*. In addition, *Abérmawdd* was anglicised to **Barmouth** — the replacement of Welsh *mawdd* by the English near-homophone *mouth* resulting in a concealed tautological hybrid, i.e. (*a*)*ber*, 'mouth', plus *mouth*.

Names like these provide many fascinating insights, and their importance in the context of place-name study as a whole will hardly need emphasising. By their very nature, however, most of them tend to be misleading even where they are not altogether obscure or meaningless; they will therefore be avoided during the rest of this chapter and in the next. In both chapters, names are dealt with on the basis that they make good sense as they stand — and also (for the most part) clearly illustrate the language-mechanisms outlined in the Introduction.

(There are cases, of course, where the modern forms of names may represent rationalisations of older obscurities; but such cases — where they exist — are not our present concern.)

Single-Element

The basis of almost every place-name consists of a common noun (Welsh *enw cyffredin*, see Chapter 5), and sometimes such a noun stands alone — denoting a locality or (far more often) a particular feature of the landscape, natural or man-made. Not a few names in Wales belong to this single-element category, for which the term 'simplex' (as distinct from 'compound') is normally used; but their simple structure is not necessarily a guide to their antiquity.

Single elements may or may not be preceded by the definite

article — there is no *in*definite article as such in Welsh — which does not count as an element in its own right; indeed, there appears to be some doubt as to when the article first came to be used in Brythonic-based place-names. Where it appears before feminine singular elements, lenition of the following initial occurs regularly; however, one needs to be on the alert for instances like **Fron** (Clw), 'Hillside' (*bron*), where the lenition of *b-* to *f-* is an indication that the article was once present but has since been lost. (Such instances are more common among names with more than one element.)

Masculines without the article include **Bryn** (Gla, Gwy). 'Hill', **Bwlch** (Pow), 'Pass', **Cefn** (Clw), 'Ridge', **Dyffryn** (Gla, Gw, Gwy), 'Valley', **Cloddiau** (Pow), 'Embankments' or 'Ditches' (plural of *clawdd*), and **Sarn** (Pow), 'Causeway'. Among feminines either not showing or not subject to lenition are **Ffridd** (Clw), 'Mountain pasture', **Rhyd** (Gwy), 'Ford', **Caerau** (Gla), 'Forts', **Rhos** (Dyf, Gla), 'Moorland', **Magwyr** (Gw), 'Wall', and **Ynys** (Gwy), 'Island' or 'Water-meadow'.

Masculines preceded by the article include **Y Bala** (Gwy), 'The river-outlet' (from a lake), **Y Betws** (Gw, Gwy), 'The chapel of ease', **Yr Ystrad** (Gla), 'The vale', **Y Porth** (Gla), 'The harbour' (note that in **Y Borth**, Dyfed, *porth* is treated as feminine), and **Y Cymer** (Gla), 'The confluence'. We also find the feminines **Y Foel** (Gwy, Pow), 'The bare hill', **Y Glog** (Dyf, Pow), 'The crag', **Y Garn** (Dyf), 'The cairn', **Y Faenor** (Pow), 'The chief's residence' (*maenor*), **Y Fan** (Gla, Pow), 'The peak' (*ban*), **Y Rhiw** (Gwy), 'The slope', **Y Wern** (Clw), 'The alder swamp' and **Y Waun** (Clw), 'The meadow' or 'The moor'. Like Fron are **Garreg** (Gwy), '(The) rock' (*carreg*) and **Gelli** (Dyf), '(The) grove, copse' (*celli*).

Adjectival names of one element are very rare, but it is worth noting **Mawr** (Gla), 'Great', and **Diffwys** (Gwy), 'Steep (place)', i.e. precipice.

Ownership

Sometimes the single element consists of a personal name, to which a suffix has been added giving the sense 'pertaining to', 'belonging to', 'territory or place of'.

Thus **Brycheiniog** is made up of the personal name Brychan (from Irish Broccan), plus -*iog*, the meaning being 'Territory of Brychan'. (The territorial name was taken into English as **Brecknock**, the personal name as **Brecon**.) The same ending is found in **Tudweiliog** (Gwy), 'Territory of Tudwal'. It will be noted that in both names the original -*a*- sounds have been changed to -*ei*-; this change is due to the process known as *i*-affection.

The same process has been at work in **Cedweli** (Gwy) — usually pronounced **Cydweli** — consisting of Cadwal plus -*i*, 'Territory of Cadwal', and in **Ceri** (Pow), 'Territory of Car' (both these names formerly denoted *cymydau*, 'commotes', ancient units of land within the larger units called *cantrefi*, 'cantrefs', 'hundreds'). Here the -*a*- sounds have been changed to -*e*- sounds; and the -*e*- sounds have arisen too in **Ceredigion**, 'Territory of Ceredig'. In this case the -*i*- of -*ig*-, earlier -*ic*- has caused the changes to the internal vowels of a personal name stemming from an original *Coroticos* or *Caraticos* (-*ion* being the 'ownership' suffix).

Place names of this type are well evidenced from the Romano-British period — though it is not always clear whether a given suffix relates to a person or a thing. Thus *Eburacum* (**York**), showing the suffix *-āco-*, may mean either 'Place of Eburos' or 'Place of yew(s)' (Celtic *eburo-*). The -*āco*- suffix gave later -*og*, which is found in *Caer Efrog* (the Welsh name for York), and also in such Welsh place-name components as *crafog, ysgallog, mawnog, rhedynog, celynog* — referring to garlic, thistles, peat, bracken, holly respectively.

Double-Element

Names consisting of two elements are rather more awkward to deal with. First, of course, there is the fact that in Welsh — unlike in English — qualifying elements (adjectives, nouns) may precede *or* follow the elements they qualify; in either case the rules of lenition come into play. And secondly, in Welsh — unlike in Cornish or Breton, where names of more than two elements are rare — certain double-element formations have a bearing on those involving three or four elements. Both factors need to be taken into account in looking for a system of classification.

For the purposes of the present book, symbols are employed as a means of overcoming this problem. While doubtless open to criticism, it does have some logical justification, as well as making for economy and visual simplicity — not least where names of the longer variety are concerned.

No matter how many elements it may contain, every Welsh place-name has one principal term (a common noun), which may be symbolised by x. The principal term is sometimes qualified by an adjective, f, sometimes by another noun, f^1. Using these symbols as bases, the four different types of double-element name can be represented as follows:

fx — Adjective-qualifier plus noun, e.g. **Gwynfryn** (Clw)

f^1x — Noun-qualifier plus noun, e.g. **Croesty** (Pow)

xf — Noun plus adjective-qualifier, e.g. **Bryngwyn** (Gw)

xf^1 — Noun plus noun-qualifier, e.g. **Tŷ-croes** (Gla, Môn)

Compounds

The names Gwynfryn, 'White hill', 'Fair hill' (fx) and Croesty, 'Cross (roads) house' (f^1x) above represent what are formally known as 'proper compounds', in which initial lenition in the second element is automatic (in Croesty, the lenited -d- of -ty has been unvoiced after -s). These are the only two types of compound known from the Romano-British period, where (for example) we find fx represented by *Letoceto*, **lēto-*, 'grey' plus **cēto(n)*, 'wood', and f^1x by *Moriduno*, **mori*, 'sea' plus **dūno(n)*, 'fort'.

It is clear that the order of words in an fx compound can be inverted without change of meaning — i.e. Gwynfryn (fx) is equivalent to Bryngwyn (xf). By contrast, if the order of words in an f^1x compound is inverted so as to create another proper compound, the meaning is inverted while the form stays the same — i.e. if we invert Croesty, which really signifies 'Of-cross (roads) house', the notional name **Tŷgroes* would signify 'Of-house cross (roads)'; the meanings are exactly opposite, although both

21

compounds are (by definition) of the same form f^1x. (In Brythonic personal-name f^1x compounds such as *Maglocunos*, 'Prince hound', *Cunomaglos*, 'Hound prince', the word-order was apparently invertible without loss of meaning because the nouns in question stood in apposition.)

The true equivalent of an f^1x compound is a different kind of compound of the type xf^1 — that is, Croesty, 'Of-cross (roads) house' is equivalent to Tŷ-croes, 'House of-cross (roads)'; except in rare ambiguous cases, this rule holds good. Formally, compounds of the xf and xf^1 type are known as 'improper compounds'; and it seems that place names coined on their pattern became common only after the Romano-British period (though presumably before the migrations to Brittany, since many examples of both types are found in Breton).

Romano-British *Duroverno*, 'Fort (of) alder-swamp' (the original name of **Canterbury** K), together with one or two other names with **duro-* as first element, suggests that xf^1 compound names at least were not unknown in Roman Britain; and O.J. Padel, in his *Cornish Place-Name Elements* (1985), suggests that Welsh names such as **Pen-tyrch** (Gla) — 'Head (of) boar' — may also date from earlier than the 5th century. However, apart from the **duro-* names, no Romano-British improper-compound names (Dr Padel's 'name-phrases') are on record.

In spite of this fact, it can be seen that Welsh, Cornish and Breton names of xf and xf^1 compound type are logically implicit in the older fx and f^1x compounds. No answer as to *why* one type came to supplant — or supplement — the other at a given point in time can possibly be attempted here.

Type fx

The prototype example mentioned in the last section was *Letoceto*, 'Grey wood', and it is an interesting one for two reasons. First, it was taken over by the Anglo-Saxons at its Primitive Welsh stage of development (in the first half of the 7th century) and, in the form recorded c. 730 as *Liccid-/Lyccid-*, provided the first element of

Lichfield (St). And secondly, in the name **Llwytgoed** (Gla), the original Brythonic elements are shown normally developed into Modern Welsh.

There is no shortage of other *fx* names in Wales. However (and this applies to Llwytgoed itself), their structure alone does not constitute proof of their antiquity, since some of them at least may have been formed on the principle of analogy. With this proviso, *fx* compound names are always *likely* to be old.

Like Llwytgoed are **Brithdir** (Gla, Gwy, Pow), 'Speckled land' (*tir*), **Y Dduallt** (Gwy, Pow), 'The black hillside', **Y Gamriw** (Pow), 'The crooked ascent', (*rhiw*), **Garwfynydd** (Gwy), 'Rugged mountain', **Glasfryn** (Clw), 'Green or blue hill', **Gloywlyn** (Gwy), 'Bright lake or glen' (*llyn, glyn*), **Gwastadros** (Gwy), 'Level plain', **Hirfynydd** (Gla), 'Long mountain' (already mentioned), **Moelfre** (Clw, Gwy, Pow, Môn), 'Bare hill' (*bre*), **Rhuddlan** (Clw), 'Red bank' (*glan*), and **Ucheldre** (Gwy, Pow), 'High hamlet'.

Among names associated with water we find **Camlan** (Gwy), 'Crooked bank' (a river name which, formally, is the Modern Welsh descendant of **camboglann-*) **Gwenlais** (Dyf), 'White or fair stream' (*glais*), **Gwenddwr** (Pow), 'Fair water', **Oernant** (Gwy), 'Cold stream', and **Sychnant** (Gwy, Pow), 'Dry stream' (this could mean 'dried-up' or 'dry in summer').

It will be noted that initial lenition in second elements (wherever applicable) is regular. In **Dugoedydd** (Dyf), 'Black trees', the adjective is singular and the noun plural; this, too, is quite regular in proper compounds of the 'strict' kind (see Chapter 4).

As already mentioned, the adjective *hen*, 'old', 'ancient', is one of a handful which invariably precede their nouns, thus forming proper compounds. Among place-names containing *hen* are **Henfeddau** (Dyf), 'Ancient graves' (plural of *bedd*), **Yr Hengoed** (Gla), 'The old wood', and **Henllan** (Clw, Dyf), 'Old church' (note that, after -*n*, *l*- lenited to *ll*- reverts to *l*-). In **Hen Gastell** (Pow), 'Old stronghold', the proper compound is of the 'loose' kind (Chapter 4).

Although numerals seldom form proper compounds with nouns, they do precede them and — in the case of *dau* (feminine *dwy*), 'two', and the masculine form *tri*, 'three' — are followed by initial mutations. Among *fx* place-names in this category are **Dwyran** (Môn), 'Two portions' (*rhan*, probably a portion of land), **Deunant** (Clw), 'Two streams' (note vowel mutation of *-au-* to *-eu-*), **Trichrug** (Dyf) and **Trichrugiau** (Pow), both 'Three mounds' (note that *tri* changes *c-* to *ch-*, this change being known as 'spirant' mutation), **Pedair-ffordd** (Pow), 'Four roads' (*pedair* is the feminine form of *pedwar*), **Pumsaint** (Dyf), 'Five saints' and **Saith Maen** (Pow), 'Seven stones'.

Welsh nouns after numerals do not normally take the plural form, so that Trichrugiau above provides an exception — *crugiau* being the plural of *crug*.

Type f¹x

Romano-British prototypes are fairly plentiful, more than 20 being on record from various parts of the island. Of these *f¹x* names, *Eposessa*, 'Horse seat', 'Horse stall(s)', and **Nemetobala*, perhaps 'Sanctuary hill', possibly denoted sites in Wales. A third, *Moriduno* (see above), 'Sea fort', was used for two different places, of which one is known to have been the Roman fort and city at **Carmarthen**, Welsh **Caerfyrddin**, capital of the *Demetae* tribe.

In the name Caerfyrddin, the element *caer*, 'fort', 'city' is a late addition. The development of *Moriduno* itself was to **Moriddin*, **Mor'ddin*, finally *Merddin* — or, with reduction of the vowel in the first syllable, *Myrddin*; the prefixing of *caer* then caused *m-* to be lenited to *f-*. The seer of Arthurian legend, Merddin, was said to have been first discovered at Caerfyrddin (Old Welsh *Cair Merdin*), because the city-name was ready-made for such an association; English *Merlin* is simply a corruption (*via* its latinized form) of Merddin, the personal name. The regional name **Dyfed**, incidentally, shows natural development of the stem **Demet-* in *Demetae*.

Returning to further examples of *f¹x* names in Wales, these include **Bugeildy** (Pow), 'Shepherd house' (note the change of *-ai-* to *-ei-* within the compound form), **Llaethdy** (Pow), 'Milk house',

24

i.e. 'Dairy' (compare Romano-British *Lactodoro*, probably 'Milk fort'), **Llechryd** (Dyf, Gw, Pow), 'Stone ford', **Maendy** (Gla, Gw), 'Stone house', **Y Maerdy** (Clw, Gla, Gw), 'The steward house', 'Mayor house', **Mochdre** (Clw, Pow), 'Pig hamlet', **Mwynglawdd** (Clw), 'Ore bank', **Mynachdy** (Dyf), 'Monk house', and **Yr Wyddgrug** (Clw), 'The burial mound' (*gŵydd* plus *crug*).

Among water-associated names are **Cadnant** (Clw, Gwy, Môn), 'Battle stream', **Crafnant** (Gwy), 'Garlic stream', **Gronant** (Clw), 'Gravel stream', **Hafnant** (Gwy), 'Summer stream', **Marchnant** (Dyf, Pow), 'Horse stream', and **Migneint** (Clw, Gwy), 'Bog streams' (*mign*, 'bog' plus *neint*, a plural of *nant*).

Other possible candidates are **Bolgoed** (Gla, Pow), 'Belly wood' (i.e. wood in a hollow), **Cilfynydd** (Gla), 'Corner mountain' or 'Source (of river) mountain', and **Fochriw** (Gla), 'Cheek slope' (*boch*, 'cheek', with loss of the definite article).

As with *fx* names, the form of these *f¹x* specimens does not itself guarantee a pedigree stretching back to the Romano-British period, since the analogical principle may also apply here. Compounds could be formed at any period; and the cause of lenition in the second elements of genuinely old compounds (i.e. the presence between the two elements of a 'composition vowel' such as *-o-*) would not have been relevant after about the mid-6th century.

Type xf

As stated earlier, there are no Romano-British prototypes. Continental forms such as *Pennovindos*, which at first sight appear to mean 'Head white' (= 'White head'), are perhaps more likely to mean 'White-head*ed*', i.e. 'White *as regards* head', which is not quite the same thing. This kind of formation may explain **Pengam** (Gla), which looks like a genuine proper compound with the sense 'Crooked *as regards* head' (hence change by lenition of *-cam* to *-gam* in the second element following the masculine *pen*). A name of this kind is wholly adjectival, i.e. a noun *x*, such as *bryn*, *mynydd* etc., is understood but not actually expressed.

In *xf* names of the improper compound variety ('name-phrases'), lenition is not always regular in that adjectives are sometimes found with lenited initial after nouns normally counted as masculine, which ought not to occur. Examples here include **Bryn-ddu** (Môn), 'Hill black', **Cefn Fanog** (Pow), 'Ridge speckled' (*manog*), **Mynyddfawr** (Gwy), 'Mountain great', and some others. Likewise, there are occasions when the initial after feminine nouns fails to show lenition as expected, e.g. **Bron-gwyn** (Dyf), 'Hill fair, white', **Caer Du** (Pow), 'Fort black', **Carn Briw** (Dyf), 'Cairn broken', and **Eglwys-bach** (Clw), 'Church small' (contrast **Eglwys-fach** in Dyfed) — to cite only a few.

In certain cases a noun was feminine in Middle Welsh, but became masculine in Modern Welsh; one such is *llys*, 'court', so we find **Llys-wen** (Pow), 'Court white, fair', which may therefore pre-date the 15th century. In other cases — as with *llyn*, 'lake' — a noun may count as masculine in one area but feminine in another; thus **Llyn Mawr** (Pow) stands beside **Llyn Fawr** (Gla), both signifying 'Lake large'. Other nouns which (in place-names at least, and for whatever reason) tend to show gender-fluctuation include *craig*, 'rock', *moel* '(bare) hill', and *nant*, 'stream'. These are worth mentioning here since lenition beside non-lenition will inevitably show up most clearly in *xf* and *xf¹* types.

There is an abundance of both types in Wales, so it will be possible (and sensible) to present only a cross-section — some being chosen in order to illustrate particular points.

Names of *xf* type in which *x* is masculine include **Bryn-teg** (Clw, Môn), 'Hill fair', **Capel Uchaf** (Clw, Gwy), 'Chapel higher, highest' (in situation), **Cefn Blewog** (Dyf), 'Ridge grassy' (literally 'hairy'), **Comin Coch** (Pow), 'Common (land) red' (*comin* is a loan-term of Anglo-French provenance), **Llyn Cau** (Gwy), 'Lake hollow', **Llyn Dwfn** (Dyf), 'Lake deep', **Mynydd Crwn** (Dyf), 'Mountain round(ed)', and **Tircanol** (Gla), 'Land central'. An example of a masculine plural with a plural adjective is **Bryniau Duon** (Gwy), 'Hills black'.

Among feminines are **Carreg-lefn** (Môn), 'Stone smooth', feminine form of *llyfn*), **Y Darren Felen** (Pow), 'The precipice yellow, tawny' (feminine form of *melyn*), **Derwen-gam** (Dyf), 'Oak crooked', **Esgair Fraith** (Dyf), 'Slope or ascent speckled' (feminine form of *brith*), **Felinganol** (Dyf), 'Mill central' (*canol*, with probable loss of the definite article), **Foel Frech** (Clw), '(Bare) hill speckled' (*brych*, also with loss of the article), **Foel Gron** (Gwy), '(Bare) hill round' (*crwn*), **Llan-teg** (Dyf), 'Church or enclosure fair' (note the lack of lenition), **Moel Goedog** (Gwy), 'Hill woody', **Nantgaredig** (Dyf), 'Stream beloved', **Porth-gain** (Dyf), 'Harbour fine', **Trefechan** (Dyf), 'Hamlet small' (*bychan*), and **Ynys-boeth** (Gla), 'Island or water-meadow warm'.

In **Cerrig Duon** (Clw), 'Rocks black', **Creigiau Llwydion** (Clw), 'Rocks grey', and **Perthillwydion** (Clw), 'Hedges/Bushes grey', feminine plural nouns are accompanied by plural adjectives (with, of course, no initial lenition).

It may be that in some place-names showing a lenited initial letter, but no definite article, the first element had already become obsolete in everyday speech; so that the element in its *lenited* form was used (mistakenly) to coin other names. Particularly relevant here are **Gelli** names, from *celli*, 'grove', 'copse', since the original (unlenited) form is almost never found either as a first element or indeed as a single element.

Type xf[1]

Again — with the exception of names containing **duro-*, 'fort', 'walled town' as first element — Romano-British prototypes are lacking; although, as stated, it is possible to envisage such forms as (for example), **Pennon Torcī*, 'Head of-boar', Welsh Pen-tyrch (with *-o-* changed to *-y-* through *i-* affection); this would account for **Pen-tyrch** (Gla) and **Pentyrch** (Pow).

Names of xf[1] type in which x is masculine include **Bryncroes** (Gwy), 'Hill (of) cross', **Brynbeddau** (Dyf), 'Hill (of) graves, sepulchres', **Bryn y Fawnog** (Pow), 'Hill (of) the peat-bog' (*mawnog*, feminine, with *m-* lenited to *f-* after the definite article), **Cae Maen** (Gla), 'Field (of) stone' (ancient site), **Cwm Meillionen** (Gwy), 'Valley (of) clover', **Cyrn y Brain** (Clw), 'Horns (pointed

27

rocks) (of the) crows' (plural of *brân*), **Dinas Brân** (Clw), 'Fort (of) crow' (or of Brân, personal name), **Dyffryn Edeirnion** (Gwy), 'Valley (of) Edeirnion' (personal name, from Romano-British **Eterniānus*), **Ffair-rhos** (Dyf). 'Fair or mart (of) moorland', **Godir-y-bwch** (Dyf), 'Lowland (of) the buck', **Gwernesgob** (Pow), 'Alder-swamp (of) bishop' (*esgob*, from Latin *episcopus*), **Llwynpiod** (Dyf), 'Grove or bush (of) magpie', **Maesycymer** (Gw), Plain or field (of) the confluence' — and, of course, a great many others.

The name **Pengelli** (Gla) is interesting in that *c*- is lenited to *g*- after the masculine *pen*, which as a noun means 'head', 'top', 'end', and, as an adjective, 'chief'. Thus the name could either be of xf^l type — 'End (of) grove' — with irregular lenition, or it could represent a proper compound (fx) — 'Chief grove' — with regular lenition in the second element.

Names in which *x* is feminine singular normally show initials of the second element lenited regularly. Again, names formed on this pattern are extremely numerous, and the following represent no more than a sample: **Carnedd Ddafydd** (Gwy), 'Mountain (of) David', **Carn Ferched** (Dyf), 'Cairn (of) maidens' (plural of *merch*), **Cors Geirch** (Gwy), 'Fen (of) oats', **Craig Dwrch** (Gwy), 'Rock (of) boar' (*twrch*), **Crib y Ddysgl** (Gwy), 'Crest (of) the dish or cup' (*dysgl*, with *d*- lenited after the definite article), **Drefelin** (Gwy), 'Hamlet (of) mill' (here the definite article has been lost before *tre*), **Eisteddfa Gurig** (Dyf), 'Resting-place (of) Curig' (the saint), **Ffynnon-ddrain** (Dyf), 'Well or spring (of) thorns' (plural of *draen*), **Llanfedw** (Gla), 'Church (of) birch-trees' (*bedw*), and **Ynysforgan** (Gla), 'Island or water-meadow of Morgan'.

There are also, of course, many xf^l place-names with *x* feminine where the rules of lenition are not relevant, e.g. **Caer Einon (Pow), 'Fort (of) Einon'**, **Llan-saint** (Dyf), 'Church (of) saints', and a host of others.

Triple-Element

Of the eight workable combinations, by far the most common are the four in which the principal noun-term, x, stands first, followed by the element-groupings (fx), (f^1x), (xf) and (xf^1), which can be placed in brackets as shown. In fact it is rare to find the double-element groupings, fx, f^1x, xf and xf^1 followed by a secondary noun-element, (x), standing on its own.

Here are examples of each of the combinations:

(1) **Llechwedd Hirgoed** (Pow), 'Slope (of) long wood', $x + (fx)$
(2) **Penbuallt** (Pow), 'Top (of) cow pasture', $x + (f^1x)$
(3) **Bancffosfelen** (Dyf), 'Mound of ditch yellow', $x + (xf)$
(4) **Coed-pen-maen** (Gla), 'Wood (of) head (of) stone', $x + (xf^1)$
(5) ? $fx + (x)$
(6) ? $f^1x + (x)$
(7) **Castellnewydd Emlyn** (Dyf), 'Castle new (of) Emlyn', $xf + (x)$
(8) **Llanddewi Gaer** (Dyf), 'Church (of) Dewi (of) fort', $xf^1 + (x)$

Note that, in (7), *Emlyn* is a region (cantref), not a person.

Readers are reminded that the symbolism is purely a device for sorting elements into their constituent parts, providing models which facilitate translation. Obviously enough, it cannot reveal anything about the chronological order in which elements were assigned — where, that is, names were not coined as complete units. Thus Llechwedd Hirgoed is symbolised by $x + (fx)$, with x standing for the principal term, Llechwedd; but of itself this does not tell us whether the whole name is a conflation of originally distinct elements, or — if so — which one first saw the light as a selected denotative. In most cases, only historical research can solve such problems.

Meanwhile it will be seen that, for whatever reason, fx and f^1x compounds of the Romano-British type are not found at all as prior elements in combination.

Type x + (fx)

Among names formed on this pattern are **Brynsaithmarchog** (Gwy), 'Hill (of) seven knights', **Castelldwyran** (Dyf), 'Castle or stronghold (of) two parts', **Cefnddwysarn** (Gwy), 'Ridge (of) two causeways', **Cefn Hirfynydd** (Clw), 'Ridge (of) long mountain', **Cwm Hirnant** (Gwy), 'Valley (of) long stream', **Llanpumsaint** (Dyf), 'Church (of) five saints', **Llantrisant** (Gw), 'Church (of) three saints', **Llan y Deuddeg Saint** (Gw, Môn), 'Church (of) the 12 saints', **Llyn Rhuddnant** (Dyf), 'Lake (of) red stream or brook', **Maenor Hengoed** (Dyf), 'Chief-residence (of) old wood' (*maenor* could also be translated 'estate'), **Maenor Tegfynydd** (Dyf), 'Chief-residence (of) fair mountain', **Mynydd Llwytgoed** (Pow), 'Mountain (of) grey wood', **Nant yr Hengwm** (Clw), 'Stream (of) the old valley', and **Rhiwhiriarth** (Pow), 'Slope (of) long enclosure' (*garth*).

Both *dau* and the feminine *dwy*, 'two', have their initials lenited after the definite article; thus a lost definite article may explain the lenition after the masculine *cefn* in Cefnddwysarn above. The lack of lenition (*p-* to *b-*, *t-* to *d-*) in Llanpumsaint and Llantrisaint is to be noted, as is the unlenited *T-* after the feminine *maenor* in Maenor Tegfynydd. In all the names listed, of course, the (*fx*) elements are proper compounds, so that the initial lenition of each (*x*) is automatic — e.g. Tegfynydd (*mynydd*).

Type x + (f¹x)

The type is not well-evidenced. **Tomen y Faerdre** (Clw), 'Mound (of) the dairy hamlet' (*maerdre*), denotes an ancient site. **Tyddynllaethdy** (Môn), 'Smallholding (of) milk house' ('dairy') is on record, but appears not to have survived to the present day. Another valid example is **Mynydd Maendy** (Gla), 'Mountain (of) stone house' — but in general, names of this kind are few and far between.

Type x + (xf)

Bancffosfelen, by contrast, has numerous parallels. Among them are **Bryn-celli-ddu** (Môn), 'Hill (of) grove black' (a well-known prehistoric site), **Castell Grogwynion** (Dyf), 'Stronghold (of) pebbles white' (*gro*, 'pebbles', plus the plural of *gwyn*), **Cefnpyllauduon** (Gw), 'Ridge (of) pools or pits black' (*pwll*, plural *pyllau*), **Cilmaen-gwyn** (Gla), 'Retreat (of) stone white', **Cilymaenllwyd** (Dyf), 'Retreat (of) the stone grey', **Crug Llwyn-llwyd** (Dyf), 'Mound (of) grove grey', **Cwm-ffrwd-oer** (Pow), 'Valley (of) stream or torrent cold', **Esgair Llwyn-gwyn** (Pow), 'Slope (of) grove fair', **Ffridd Bryn-coch** (Gwy), 'Mountain-pasture (of) hill red', **Heol Porth-mawr** (Gla), 'Road (of) harbour great', and **Rhosllannerchrugog** (Clw), 'Moorland (of) glade heathery' (*llannerch*, 'glade', plus lenited *grugog*, from *grug*, 'heather').

When adjectives are used as epithets referring to persons, it is not uncommon to find them lenited even though the persons may be male, e.g. Cynfelin *Drwsgl*, 'Cynfelin the Clumsy' (*trwsgl*), Idwal *Frych*, 'Idwal the Freckled' (*brych*), Dyfnwal *Foel*, 'Dyfnwal the Bald' (*moel*), and so on. This probably explains the lenitions in place-names such as **Betws Gwerful Goch** (Gwy), 'Chapel of ease (of) Gwerful the Red' (*coch*), **Dôl Ifan Gethin** (Gwy), 'Meadow (of) Evan the Swarthy' (*cethin*), and some others.

Type x + (xf¹)

Whatever the history of their formation, there is no shortage of names on this pattern. Further examples to be added to Coed-pen-maen include **Castell Dolforwyn** (Pow), 'Stronghold (of) meadow (of) maiden' (*morwyn*), **Craig Blaen-y-cwm** (Gwy), 'Rock (of) end (of) the valley', **Cwm Gelli Iago** (Gwy), 'Valley (of) grove (of) Iago' (English 'James' — and note the lenited form of *celli*, 'grove', after the masculine *cwm*), **Fan Bwlch Chwyth** (Pow), 'Peak (of) pass of blast' (i.e. of wind — and here the definite article has probably been lost before *ban*, 'peak'), **Maestregymer** (Pow),

'Plain of hamlet (of) confluence' (*cymer*), **Penlle'rfedwen** (Gla),
'Head (of) place (of) the birch-tree' (*lle*, 'place', *bedwen*,
'birch-tree'), **Pont-rhyd-yr-ynn** (Gw), 'Bridge (of) ford (of) the
ash-trees' (*ynn*, plural of *onnen*), and **Troedrhiw-gwair** (Gw), 'Foot
(of) slope (of) hay'.

Other Types

The remaining four types of triple-element names are so sparsely
represented that they can be dealt with under a single heading. As
already mentioned, *fx* and *f¹x* compounds seem not to be used at all
as bases for extended constructions, while $xf + (x)$ and $xf¹ + (x)$
names are themselves very thin on the ground. Indeed, the only
parallel to Castellnewydd Emlyn that suggests itself is **Bryngwyn
Esgob** (Clw), 'Hill white (of) bishop', though doubtless others
exist.

The few $xf¹ + (x)$ names are mostly church-orientated. Thus we
find **Eglwys Fair y Mynydd** (Gla), 'Church (of) Mary (of) the
mountain', **Llanbadarn Fynydd** (Pow), 'Church (of) Padarn (of)
mountain' (note lenition, *mynydd* to *fynydd*), **Llandeilo Graban**
(Pow), 'Church (of) Teilo (of) corn-marigold' (*graban*, unlenited),
Llanfihangel Ystrad (Dyf), 'Church (of) Michael (of) valley', and a
handful of others — in most of which the secondary term, (*x*), has
locative force.

Note that names like **Tŷ-brith Isaf, Tŷ-brith Uchaf** (Clw),
'House mottled Lower', 'House mottled Upper', where both the
second and third elements are adjectives (the third usually with
locative force) — and which would have to be symbolised in some
such way as (*xf*)*f* — have been ignored here, although one or two
similar examples will crop up in Chapter 3.

Quadruple-Element

Here again, compounds of the *fx* and *f¹x* type seem not to feature in
prior position. There are also very few names in which a single
element, *x*, is followed by a three-element combination; they

include **Carn Penrhiw-ddu** (Dyf), 'Cairn (of) top (of) slope black', and **Carnpenrhiwllwydog** (Dyf), 'Cairn (of) top (of) slope greyish'. In the case of **Garndolbenmaen** (Gwy), 'Cairn (of) meadow (of) head (of) stone', Dolbenmaen is the local parish name; note that *carn* (feminine) is lenited to *garn*, perhaps signalling a lost definite article, but that *dol* is not lenited to *ddol*.

The vast majority of other quadruple-element names are, once again, church-orientated. Classifiable as $xf^l + (fx)$ are **Llanfair Rhuddallt** (Gwy), 'Church (of) Mary (of) red slope', and **Llansanffraid Deuddwr** (Pow), 'Church (of) Saint-Ffraid (of) two rivers' (Welsh *Ffraid* is the English 'Bridget' or 'Bride'). Under $xf^l + (xf^l)$ are found **Llanfihangel Brynpabuan** (Pow), 'Church (of) Michael (of) hill (of) Pabuan', and the (non-ecclesiastical) **Pen-bont Rhydybeddau** (Dyf), 'End (of) bridge (of) ford (of) the graves'. **Llanfair Nant-gwyn** (Dyf), 'Church (of) Mary (of) stream fair', **Llanfihangel Cwm Du** (Pow), 'Church (of) Michael (of) valley black', and **Llanarmon Mynydd Mawr** (Clw), 'Church (of) Garmon (of) mountain great', are all $xf^l + (xf)$. Lastly, $xf + (xf^l)$ names seem to be restricted to **Mynydd Bach Trecastell** (Pow), 'Mountain small (of) hamlet (of) castle', and **Drenewydd Gelli Farch** (Gw), 'Hamlet new (of) grove (of) horse' (*march*) — this being the English **Shirenewton**.

In **Maenor Cefndaufynydd** (Dyf), 'Estate (of) ridge (of) two mountains', $x + (x + fx)$, the first element x may not be organic; and in fact, with the exception of those in which *llan*, 'church' is the first element, quadruple-element names are not all that common.

This brings us nearly to the end of our investigation into the patterns of Welsh place-names construction (and it is hoped that the use of symbols has proved to be of some assistance here). However, before concluding the chapter with a look at the use of prepositions, it is necessary to put in an extra word or two about compounds (proper and improper).

Some readers may feel that place names like Llaethdy ought not to be treated as double-element constructions, on the grounds that *llaethdy*, 'dairy', would normally count as a single word in everyday speech; and the same might be felt about (for example), **Hendre**

(Clw, Gla), literally 'Old hamlet', 'Old homestead' (since *hendre* is now established as a single word with the sense 'winter dwelling'), **Pentre** (Clw, Gwy), literally 'End (of) hamlet' (*pentref* now having the sense 'village'), **Penrhyn** (Dyf, Gwy, Môn), 'Chief point' ('promontory'), **Pentir** (Gwy), 'End (of) land' ('headland') — and various other names of this type.

In translation it is perhaps of no great importance whether we think of — say — **Rhandirganol** (Dyf), 'Region central' (*canol*) as a double- or triple-element construction. However, it is of *semantic* interest that *rhandir* consists of *rhan*, 'share' plus *tir*, 'land' (comprising either a proper or an improper compound, 'shareland' or 'share of-land'), and of *historical* interest that this 'share' may have contained four *tyddynau*, 'farms', 'small-holdings'. In short, words of compound nature may have rather more to tell us than is conveyed by the meanings they have come to acquire nowadays.

Prepositions

One preposition that needs careful watching is *yn*, 'in', since it not only causes changes (the 'nasal mutation') to certain following consonants but is itself also subject to change.

So in **Llanfair-yng-Nghedewain** (Pow), 'Church (of) Mary in Cedewain' (an old commote), initial *c-* of the last element has been altered to *ngh-*, while *yn* has become *yng*. Another example is **Llanfair-yng-Nghornwy** (Môn), 'Church (of) Mary in Cornwy'.

In **Llanfair-ym-Muallt** (Pow), 'Church (of) Mary in Buallt', the *b-* of *buallt*, 'cow-pasture' has become *m-* after *yn*, which has itself become *ym*. (This is the English **Builth**, which retains original *b-*.)

Likewise *g-* is changed to *ng-*, as in **Llanfihangel-yng-Ngwynfa** (Pow), 'Church (of) Michael in Gwynfa' ('Fair place'?). Note that here, too, *yn* becomes *yng*.

In **Y Castell Coch ym Mhowys** (Pow), 'The stronghold red in Powys', we see that initial *P-* of **Powys** is changed to *Mh-*, while *yn* changes to *ym*. (The name Powys itself derives from Latin **Pāgē(n)ses*, 'dwellers in the country-district', *pagus*.)

The nasal mutation of *t-* is to *nh-*, and this is found in

Llanfihangel-yn-Nhywyn (Môn), 'Church (of) Michael in Tywyn'; note that *yn* is unchanged.

Other common prepositions are *is* and *islaw*, 'below', *uwch* and *uwchlaw*, 'above' (none of these causes mutations), and *dan*, 'under' (soft mutation). These prepositions are represented respectively in **Is-y-coed** (Pow), 'Below the wood', **Islaw'r-dref** (Gwy), 'Below the hamlet', **Uwchygarreg** (Pow), 'Above the rock', **Uwchlaw'r Coed** (Gw, Pow), 'Above the wood', and **Dan-yr-Ogof** (Pow), 'Under the cave'.

Chapter 3

Some Leading Themes

With the help of an improvised but not — it is hoped — too cumbersome a method, the aim in Chapter 2 was to show how Welsh place-names are built up, and for the most part the examples cited there were chosen with no other end in view. However, it is plain that these examples express a wide range of themes — so wide, in fact, that in the present chapter it provides specific contexts within which further names may be considered, their structure no longer being of prime concern.

As is also the case in England, we find extensive reference to prominent features of the landscape, together with frequent reference to particular types of trees and plants; animals, too, are well documented. There is no shortage of personal names, although (with the notable exception of saints' names, which, not unnaturally, occur most frequently in association with *llan*, 'church') these play a rather less important rôle than they do in England. Many names refer directly to human occupations and activities, while others mirror human beliefs or superstitions.

Again as in England, some of the recurrent themes are found in place names of the 'habitation' type — Welsh *tre(f)* and *pentre(f)* answering in large measure to Old English *tūn* and *hām*, Old Scandinavian *bý*, etc. So — for example — Welsh **Tre-wern** (Pow), 'Hamlet (of) alders', and **Pentre-cwm** (Dyf), 'Village (of) valley' are closely echoed in meaning by English **Alderton** (Sa, Sf) and **Denham** (Sf) respectively (the latter containing Old English *denu*, 'valley', plus *hām*). However, it is probably true to say that, in relation to the whole body of Welsh place-names, *tre(f)* and *pentre(f)* occur less frequently as elements than do *tūn*, *hām* and *bý* in England.

Meanwhile both countries can show large numbers of names which, although known technically as 'nature-names', nevertheless refer to inhabited places. Thus **Maesteg** (Gla), 'Field or plain fair', and **Cwm-du** (Gla), 'Valley black' — both names of villages — find near-exact parallels in English **Fairfield** (Db, K), containing Old English *feld*, and **Blackden** (Chs); and of course, examples could be multiplied.

There are, then, similarities as well as differences between the place-names of Wales and England. What, perhaps, gives Welsh names their unique charm and beauty is the expansiveness of their forms, combined with the melodious rhythms inherent in the language itself. There are no real English equivalents of — say — **Cwys yr Ychen Bannog** (Dyf), 'Furrow of the horned oxen', or **Moel y Cerrigduon** (Gwy, Pow), 'Bare hill of the black rocks'; only a native Welsh-speaker can convey the full flavour of names like these and countless others.

Trees and Plants

Beginning with trees, it should perhaps be mentioned that most of the words denoting them have two forms, a singular with the ending *-en* and a collective/plural without it — e.g. *bedwen*, 'birch tree', *bedw*, 'birches', 'birch wood'. This is well illustrated by **Penlle'rfedwen** and **Llanfedw** (which may be remembered from Chapter 2) as also by **Bedw** (Dyf), a river name, **Fedw** (Pow), and **Caerfedwen** (Clw).

The holly tree has given its name to **Celynnen** (Gw) and **Cilygelynnen** (Dyf) — first element *cil*, 'nook', 'corner'. **Ysgawen** (Clw) means 'Elder tree', while **Helyg** (Clw), 'Willows' is the name of a lake or tarn (*llyn*).

There can be little doubt that Christian associations were sometimes foisted onto places of pagan origin; thus **Castell Collen** (Pow), site of a Roman fort, may mean either 'Fort (of) hazel tree' or 'Fort (of) Collen', this being the name of a 7th-century saint — compare **Llangollen** (Clw), where the same ambiguity exists. Meanwhile **Collfryn** (Pow) is 'Hazel hill'.

The hawthorn features in **Y Ddraenen Wen** (Gla) — literally 'The thorn white' — while in **Ffawyddog** (Pow), '(Place of) beech trees', we see the ending -og (from *-āco-) which was explained in Chapter 2 and which in turn also explains the river name **Celynnog** (Gwy), '(Place of) holly trees'. **Nant Cerdinen** (Dyf) is 'Stream (of) rowan', and another word for this tree, *criafolen*, is found in **Waun y Griafolen** (Gwy), 'Meadow (of) the rowan'.

Mention of fruit trees is comparatively rare, but **Blaenrhiwafallen** (Dyf) signifies 'Head (of) slope (of) apple tree' (*afallen*), while the medlar (*ceri*) seems to have given its name to the river **Ceri** (Dyf).

Turning to other types of plant, **Cegidog** (Clw) is '(Place of) hemlock', and **Cegidfa** (Pow) has the same meaning. (The ending -*fa* here is the lenited form of **magos*, 'field', 'place', the ending -*os* having been lost.) **Ystumcegid** (Gwy) is 'River-bed (of) hemlock.'

Bodysgallen (Gwy) combines *bod*, 'dwelling' with *ysgallen*, 'thistle'; **Berth-lwyd** (Gla, Pow), 'Hedge/bush grey' shows *p*-lenited to *b*-, probably again through loss of the definite article. Ferns or bracken (*rhedyn*) determined the naming of **Cilrhedyn** (Dyf), rushes (*brwyn*) that of **Cefn Brwynog** (Dyf), and furze (*eithin*) that of **Cefneithin** (Dyf). Bilberries (*llus*) grew at **Bryn Llus** (Gwy), raspberries (*afan*) at **Blaenafan** (Gla) — source of the river **Afan**. **Capel Berw** (Môn) signifies 'Chapel (of) cress'.

Rivers, too, record names of plants, e.g. the **Alaw** (Môn), 'Lily', and the **Cywarch** (Gwy), 'Hemp'. Notable, however, is the comparative lack of recourse to cultivated plants as a basis of place-naming, though **Cae Ceirch** (Gwy) is 'Field (of) oats', while **Maesygwenith** (Gw) means 'Field (of) the wheat'.

(Note: It is very probable that crops feature more prominently in field-names throughout Wales, but for the most part in this book the latter have not been utilised.)

Animals

In the case of trees and plants, it is obviously reasonable to assume that they were, or indeed still are, physically present in the areas whose place-names refer to them. However, the same assumption cannot be made quite so confidently with animal and bird-names, since other possibilities have to be taken into account.

Pentyrch (Pow), for example, was mentioned in the course of the last chapter as meaning — literally — 'Head (of) boar'. But we cannot be certain whether the name resulted from the likening of a prominent natural feature to the shape of a boar's head, or whether the sense is simply 'head or headland associated with a boar or boars'. Another suggestion put forward is that names of this particular type — compare **Penanner** (Gwy), 'Head (of) heifer', **Penporchell** (Gwy), 'Head (of) pig', **Pen-hydd** (Gla), 'Head (of) stag' etc. — may stem from the practice of animal sacrifice, the animal's head being erected on a stake (sometimes to mark a meeting-place or boundary).

There are other types of name whose literal meaning presents no difficulty but whose precise implications are nevertheless obscure. For instance, at least half a dozen widely separated prehistoric sites in Wales (burial chambers, standing stones) are associated specifically with the greyhound-bitch, *miliast*, although it is not easy to say why. Examples here include **Gwâl y Filiast** (Dyf, Gla, Gw) and **Twlc y Filiast** (Gwy), *gwâl* and *twlc* both signifying 'kennel'. In addition, the male of the breed (*milgi*) is referred to in **Ffynnon Maenmilgi** (Gwy), 'Spring (of) stone (of) greyhound', so that one is tempted to suspect some arcane reason for these namings that eludes us today. (To try to explain them all in terms of fancied resemblances to greyhounds would surely be stretching coincidence too far.)

However, even allowing for this kind of uncertainty in given instances, both animals and birds are well represented in place-names. **Marchnant** (Dyf, Pow), 'Horse stream' has already been mentioned, and we also find **Castell March** (Gwy), 'Stronghold (of) horse' and **Naid-y-March** (Clw), 'Leap (of) the horse' — site of two standing stones; the plural *meirch* occurs in **Moel Meirch** (Gwy), '(Bare) hill (of) horses'. Another word denoting this animal is *ceffyl* — hence **Bryn Ceffyl** (Gwy). The colt (*ebol*) features in **Llwynyrebol** (Dyf) — *llwyn*, 'grove' — while **Blaencrugebolion** (Dyf), 'Head (of) mound (of) colts' has the plural *ebolion* as second element. The river **Caseg** (Gwy) means 'Mare'.

Carnedd y Ci (Gwy) is 'Cairn or mountain (of) the dog', the plural *cŵn* being found in **Trecŵn** (Dyf). The wolf, *blaidd*, is mentioned in **Pwll-y-blaidd** (Pow) — English **Wolfpits** — while the menace of wolf-packs may be implied in **Ffosybleiddiaid** (Dyf), 'Ditch (of) the wolves', and **Llannerchybleiddiau** (Dyf), 'Glade (of) the wolves' (note that *blaidd* has two different forms in the plural). The cat (*cath*) in **Onnen-y-gath** (Gw), English **Catsash**, was probably a wild one. **Cwrtycadno** (Dyf) is 'Court (of) the fox' — a locality-name not without charm, as is also the case with **Castell Draenog** (Dyf), 'Stronghold (of) hedgehog'. Porcine names include **Castell Moch** (Pow), 'Stronghold (of) pigs', **Braich yr Hwch** (Gwy), 'Ridge (of) the sow', and the rivers **Banw** (Pow), 'Boar' and **Beinw** (Gwy), 'Boars'. Among bovine ones are **Cil-yr-ŷch** (Pow), 'Nook (of) the ox', **Porth Ychen** (Gwy), 'Harbour (of) oxen', and **Llyn y Tarw** (Pow), 'Lake (of) the bull'.

Llechwedd Bryniau Defaid (Gwy), 'Slope (of) hills (of) sheep' has as its last element the plural of *dafad*, which can also have the more specific sense 'ewe'. **Llwyn yr Hwrdd** (Dyf) is 'Grove (of) the ram', while **Carn yr Hyrddod** (Gla), 'Cairn (of) the rams' exhibits the plural. The lake-name **Gafr** (Gwy) signifies 'Goat', the plural form appearing in **Carn y Geifr** (Pow).

Foel yr Hydd (Gwy), 'Hill (of) the stag' can be added to the ambiguous **Pen-hydd** referred to above, while *carw*, 'red deer' and its plural *ceirw* are found respectively in the lake-name **Carw** (Pow) and in **Cwmrhydyceirw** (Gla), 'Valley (of) ford (of) the red deer', — though it should be noted that the second of these two names is probably a 'puritanical' version of a correct **Cwmrhydycwrw**, 'Valley (of) ford (of) the *beer*' (*cwrw*). Finally, **Nant-y-bwch** (Gw) is 'Stream (of) the buck', and the river **Iwrch** (Clw) is the 'Roebuck'.

Birds

We have already seen a reference to the crow or raven in **Dinas Brân** (Clw) — although, as stated, Brân is also a personal name — and to this may be added **Brân** (Dyf), a river, **Cwmbrân** (Gw), and a few others. **Cyrn y Brain** (Clw), 'Horns (of) the ravens' shows the plural forms of both *brân* and of *corn*, 'horn', here probably used figuratively of a rock-shape. **Craignythygigfran** (Gwy) is 'Crag (of) nest (of) the raven' — *nyth*, 'nest', plus *cigfran*, another term for this bird.

Carngwcw (Dyf) contains the lenited form of *cwcw*, 'cuckoo' — hence 'Cairn (of) cuckoo'. An alternative term in this instance is *cog*, which is found in **Pant-y-gog** (Gla), where *pant* is 'valley', 'hollow'.

The blackbird (*mwyalch*) is linked with a cross in **Croes y Mwyalch** (Gw), and — in the plural — with a hillock in **Twyn Mwyalchod** (Clw). **Castell y Dryw** (Gla) is 'Stronghold (of) the wren', **Craig yr Eos** (Gla) is 'Rock or crag (of) the nightingale', and the peacock (perhaps brought to Britain originally by the Romans, whose word **paōnem* is behind the Welsh *paun*) frequented the wood at **Coed y Paun** (Gw). **Nant Gwennol** (Gwy, Pow) signifies 'Stream (of) swallow'. In the case of **Rhaeadr Ewynnol** (Gwy), the meaning is 'Waterfall foaming' (*ewynol*, more commonly *ewynog*); the English version — 'Swallow falls' — appears to be based on a mistaken Welsh **Rhaeadr y Wennol**, showing *gwennol* in its lenited form.

The eagle (*eryr*), hawk (*hebog*) and kite (*barcud*) have lent their names to **Allt-yr-Eryr** (Pow), **Pwll yr Hebog** (Gla) and **Cors y Barcud** (Gwy), 'Swamp (of) the kite', respectively. Freshwater and sea birds also make their appearance, the former in **Deri Garan** (Dyf), 'Oak trees (of) crane' and **Castell Crychydd** (Dyf), 'Stronghold (of) heron', the latter in **Ynysoedd Gwylanod** (Môn), 'Islands of seagulls'. **Clip y Gylfinir** (Gwy) is 'Crag (of) the curlew'. Among game birds, mention is made of the grouse in **Llyn Coch-hwyad** (Pow) — literally 'Lake (of) red duck' — and of the woodcock (*cyfyllog*) in **Ynysygyfyllog** (Gwy).

Legend and Superstition

Not surprisingly, a good many of the names with a superstitious ring to them are connected with prehistoric sites, just as in the rest of Britain; and of course, superstition and legend tend to overlap when places linked with, say, giants or witches spawn tales of deeds performed by them or against them. However, as hitherto, the purpose here is chiefly to convey the meanings of the names themselves.

Taking prehistoric sites first, the concept of the giant (*cawr*) and his grave (*bedd*) is exemplified by **Bedd y Cawr** (Clw) and — in the plural — by **Beddau'r Cewri** (Pow), 'Graves (of) the giants'. The giantess (*cawres*) has her place in the more fanciful **Barclodiad y Gawres** (Môn), where *barclodiad* signifies 'apronful' — though of what, precisely, seems uncertain, and the same applies with **Arffedogaid Y Wrach** (Clw), 'Apronful (of) the witch' (note that the *w* in the lenited *gwrach* is a consonant, not a vowel, hence *y*, not *yr*, as the preceding definite article).

Bryn-yr-Ellyllon (Clw), 'Hill (of) the goblins or fiends', is the site of a former cairn, and direct reference to another cairn (*carnedd*) is found in **Carnedd y Ddelw** (Gwy), *delw* signifying 'image', 'idol'. In the case of **Bedd Illtud** (Pow) and **Tŷ Illtud** (Pow) — where a cairn and a chamber-tomb have been dubbed 'grave' and 'house' respectively — we doubtless see once more the Christianising process at work, since Illtud is the name of a particularly well-known saint of the 6th century who came to Wales from Brittany. **Bryn yr Hen Bobl** (Môn) signifies 'Hill (of) the ancient folk' (*pobl*) — the latter being the unknown builders of the burial chamber here. In **Bedd yr Afanc** (Dyf) the word *afanc* can mean either 'beaver' or 'crocodile'; the second naming, in the sense 'water-monster', is probably indicated, as it is also in **Llyn yr Afanc** (Gwy).

Just as saints' names are occasionally found in unlikely settings, so too — perhaps inevitably — links have been created between prehistoric sites and figures from Welsh legend who are well enough known independently of them.

A good example is provided by **Dinas Emrys** (Gwy), 'Fort (of) Emrys' — the personal name here being the Modern Welsh equivalent of *Ambrosius*. Possibly the original connexion was with the 5th-century nobleman, mentioned in Chapter 1, who led the initial British resistance to the Anglo-Saxons. However, tradition holds that the fort was built with the miraculous assistance of Merlin (Myrddin); and this, apparently, is because Geoffrey of Monmouth, the 12th-century creator of Merlin in his rôle as wizard, not only attributes to him many of the feats said by Nennius (*History of the Britons*) to have been performed by the earlier leader, but also states that he (Merlin) was *also* called Ambrosius (*History of the Kings of Britain*, vi, 19). Geoffrey's famous character has likewise lent his name to **Coetan Myrddin** (Dyf) and **Carreg Fyrddin** (Dyf) — a 'quoit' and a standing stone respectively.

The number of sites in Wales named after the still more famous Arthur is too great to be listed in detail here, though it is worth noting that his sons are mentioned in **Cerrig Meibion Arthur** (Dyf), showing the plural of *mab*, 'son', and referring to a pair of standing stones. Who these sons were appears to be anybody's guess.

The Romans regarded Britain as the centre of Druidism, and it has been suggested that one of the aims behind their invasion of the island was to extirpate it once and for all. If so, their aim was duly accomplished c. 60 AD, with the wholesale massacre of the priesthood in Anglesey. Nevertheless, various prehistoric sites in both Wales and England were later — rightly or wrongly — perceived as being associated with the cult; in Wales, one such site is **Beddau'r Derwyddon** (Gwy), 'Graves of the Druids', while the singular *derwydd* is found in **Derwydd** (Dyf) and **Moel Derwydd** (Clw). It is interesting, too, that in more than one Welsh dictionary the word *dryw*, whose more usual meaning is 'wren', is also given the sense 'Druid'; and even though this may stem from a confusion, it may also, conceivably, throw fresh light on **Castell y Dryw** (Gla), already mentioned. Meanwhile **Foel Offrwm** (Gwy), 'Hill (of) sacrifice', sounds another intriguing note on which to conclude this section.

Activities

From a very early period, the use of iron in the making of tools and weapons has obviously played an important part in human affairs, and this fact is reflected in a number of place-names. **Tonyrefail** (Gla) is 'Meadow (of) the smithy' (*gefail*), and presumably there were smithies too at **Efailfach** (Gla) — *bach*, 'small' — **Efailisaf** (Gla) — *isaf*, 'lower' — and **Efailnewydd** (Gwy) — *newydd*, 'new' (and note that in these last three names the definite article has been lost).

At the beginning of Chapter 2 we saw that the name **Abergavenny** contains a Brythonic word (**gobann-*) signifying 'blacksmith', and its descendant, *gof*, is found with the same meaning in **Mynydd-y-gof** (Môn), **Nantygof** (Dyf), **Pantygof** (Dyf) - *pant*, 'hollow', 'valley' — and **Rhyd-y-gof Isaf** (Dyf) — *rhyd*, 'ford'. At **Coed-y-gof** (Gwy), charcoal for smelting may have been prepared direct from the wood (*coed*), and traces of charcoal were certainly found in the prehistoric chambers at **Cerrig-y-gof** (Dyf), 'Stones (of) the smith'.

Reference to coal (*glo*) is made in **Cwm-y-glo** (Gwy) and **Nant-y-glo** (Gw), while **Pont-y-gwaith** (Gla) is 'Bridge (of) the coal-mine'. In **Rhyd-y-mwyn** (Clw), 'Ford (of) the ore', the ore in question seems likely to be either coal or lead. **Rhydodyn** (Gwy) means 'Ford (of) lime-kiln'.

Mead (the drink) was formerly as popular in Wales as it was among the early English, and **Llannerch-y-medd** (Môn) — if this means 'Glade (of) the mead' (*medd*) — may have been a place set aside for festivities. Mead, of course, is fermented honey and water (*Domesday Book* contains specific references to the honey-renders of the Welsh inhabitants of Erging or Archenfield in Herefordshire) and it is possible that the original bees (*gwenyn*) referred to in **Gwenynoguchaf** (Pow), 'Bee-place upper', and **Llidiartygwenyn** (Gwy), 'Gate or enclosure (of) the bees', were tended by bee-keepers.

Names connected with dairy farming or animal husbandry are not infrequent, examples already met with including Llaethdy

(Pow), 'Milk house', **Bugeildy** (Pow), 'Shepherd house', and **Mochdre** (Clw, Pow), 'Pig hamlet' — all proper compounds.

Beside Llaethdy can be set **Llaethgwm** (Gwy), 'Milk valley', while in the improper compound **Cwm Llefrith** (Gwy), the second element also signifies 'milk'. **Brynmenyn** (Gla) is 'Hill (of) butter', and **Hafod y Maidd** (Clw) is 'Summer-dwelling (of) the curds-and-whey'. We also find **Nant-y-caws** (Dyf), 'Stream or valley (of) the cheese'. Reference to the all-important cow (*buwch*) is made directly in **Cas-fuwch** (Dyf), where *cas* signifies 'castle', and indirectly in **Bwlchybeudy** (Clw), 'Pass (of) the cow house'. **Craig-y-llo** (Pow) is 'Rock (of) the calf'.

Bugeildy is echoed by **Nant y Bugail** (Dyf), 'Stream (of) the shepherd' and in **Bryniau Bugeilydd** (Gwy), 'Hills (of) shepherds' — an alternative plural of *bugail* being found in **Bryn Bugeiliaid** (Pow). **Defaity** (Môn) is 'Sheep house' (properly *defeity*), while **Corlannau** (Gla) means 'Sheepfolds', as does **Ffaldau** (Gla). In **Ystrad Sheephouse** (Clw), we see an interesting Welsh-English hybrid form constructed on the Welsh pattern xf^1, with *ystrad*, 'valley' as first element. **Carn yr Hyrddod** (Gla) is 'Cairn (of) the rams' (plural of *hwrdd*), **Pwll y Myn** (Gla) 'Pool (of) the kid'. In **Rhyd-wyn** (Môn), the second element is apparently the plural of *oen*, 'lamb' — hence 'Ford (of) lambs'.

To Mochdre can be added **Castell Moch** (Clw, Pow), 'Stronghold (of) pigs', and we also find **Nantmeichiad** (Pow), 'Stream or valley (of) swineherd'.

From a very early period island exports to the Continent included cattle and hides, and long after Wales had become a separate entity, Welsh cattle-drovers continued to take their beasts to English markets; thus **Rhydeidion** (Clw), 'Ford (of) bullock' should be noted as of interest. Meanwhile it may or may not be coincidental that **Llundain-fach** (Dyf), literally 'London little', is paralleled by many **Little London** names in England; for the latter often denoted areas set aside to accommodate drovers on their way to London. For what it is worth **Tŷ-crwyn** (Pow) signifies 'House (of) hides' (plural of *croen*).

Occupations besides that of blacksmith, shepherd or swineherd are mentioned. **Maen-y-Bardd** (Gwy) is 'Stone (of) the bard', the plural *beirdd* occurring in **Pentre'r-beirdd** (Pow), 'Village (of) the bards'; and perhaps **Tre'rdelyn** (Pow), 'Hamlet (of) the harp' (*telyn*) has similar connotations. **Trefathro** (Dyf) is 'Hamlet (of) teacher' (*athro*), **Pantseiri** (Dyf) 'Hollow or valley (of) craftsmen' (plural of *saer*), **Pisgotwr** (Dyf) 'Fisherman'. **Fabrorum** (Clw) is not Welsh but Latin (genitive plural of *faber*), but there may have been a Welsh original behind this clericised name, which means '(Place) of craftsmen'. **Gwmslatter** (Gla) is possibly another Welsh-English hybrid — *cwm*, 'valley' plus English 'slater' (Middle English *sclatter*); alternatively the second element could be an occupational surname. **Trerhingyll** (Gla) signifies 'Hamlet (of) beadle' (*rhingyll*), while in **Rhydyceisiaid** (Gwy) the second element is the plural of *ceisiad*, also signifying 'beadle' (and perhaps 'tax-gatherer'). **Rhydymilwyr** (Clw, Gw) is 'Ford (of) the soldiers'.

The mill was obviously an important centre of activity, and to **Felinganol** (Dyf), already mentioned, should be added **Melindwr** (Dyf), 'Mill (of) water' — i.e. 'water-mill' — and **Felinwynt** (Dyf), 'Mill (of) wind' (*gwynt*). The grain brought to mills will have been stored in barns; so we find **Ysguboriau** (Dyf), 'Barns', the singular being found in **Ysgubor-fawr** (Dyf), 'Barn great', and **Ysgubor-y-coed** (Dyf), 'Barn (of) the wood' — compare **Melin-y-wig** (Gwy), 'Mill (of) the wood' (*gwig*). The word *pandy* (literally 'beating-house'), as in **Pandy** (Clw, Gw, Gwy, Pow) and **Tonypandy** (Gla), means 'fulling mill'.

Dolhelfa (Pow) is 'Meadow (of) hunt', **Cyfarthfa** (Gla) — literally 'Barking place' — also refers to the hunting or baiting of wild beasts by hounds or dogs, while **Nantycyndy** (Pow) is 'Stream or valley (of) the kennel' (*cyndy*, 'doghouse'). **Trecolomendy** (Clw), 'Hamlet (of) pigeon house', may reflect the keeping of pigeons for culinary purposes — a not uncommon practice in England, at least. **Rhyd-y-gwin** (Gwy), 'Ford (of) the wine' suggests use of the place by vintners. More sombre are **Rhydclafdy** (Gwy), 'Ford (of) the infirmary' (or 'lazar house'), and the *Finnaun i Clevion*, 'Well or fountain (of) the infirm or leprous ones', *cleifion*, recorded in the *Book of Llandaff*. (The last-mentioned site may have been credited with miraculous powers, or simply set aside for sick people.) Ominous-sounding, too, is **Pant Nant y Lladron** (Gwy), 'Hollow (of) stream (of) the robbers' (plural of *lleidr*).

Finally, in **Ceubalfa** (Pow), 'Ferry-boat place', **Disgwylfa** (Pow), 'Lookout place', and **Bryn y Gydfa** (Pow), 'Hill (of) the assembly place', we see again the useful suffix *-fa*, here added to *ceubal*, *disgwyl* and (lenited) *cyd* respectively.

Church and State

Christianity had taken root in Wales by the 3rd century, and, although there is uncertainty as to how it fared in the troubled period following the departure of the legions, it was re-invigorated during the latter half of the 5th century from three principal sources.

In the southern half of the country, the Irish Brychan (Chapter 2) established a Christian dynasty which lasted at least three generations, while in the north the pattern was reproduced on a more enduring scale by the family of Cunedda — who, it is said, came to Anglesey from Strathclyde. And thirdly, a vital impetus was provided by missionaries from Brittany and Gaul. (It is possible, too, that the flow of refugees escaping westwards from the Anglo-Saxon menace included Christian elements.)

Until well into the 8th century the Welsh church remained independent of that in England, which owed its conversion almost exclusively to the work of Augustine and his successors, sponsored by the see of Rome. Subsequently, English influence increased — more so, of course, after the Norman conquest, when barons and bishops established a strong physical presence in Wales. This is why so many *Llan-* names are seen to commemorate saints drawn from the Roman calendar.

In strict contrast, a place-name having *Llan-* as its first element and a Celtic saint's name as its second indicates either that the place in question was believed to have a direct connexion with the saint (such belief was frequent) or that it was named in his honour. Claims to direct connexions usually depend more on tradition than on positive evidence; but there is equally no proof that the saints themselves were not real people.

Among those usually ascribed to the house of Brychan were Cynog, Cynidr and Dingad, whose memory lives on in **Llangynog** (Dyf, Pow), **Llangynidr** (Pow), and **Llanddingad** (Gw). The 'resting-place' (*merthyr*) of Cynog is fixed at **Merthyr Cynog** (Pow), where he was reputedly murdered by the Anglo-Saxons. Also prominent in this dynasty was Tudwal, who — as we have seen — gave his name to **Tudweiliog** (Pow).

Cunedda's line included Teilo, also met with earlier in **Llandeilo Graban** (Pow) but more especially linked by tradition with **Llandeilo Fawr** (Gwy); Mabon, as in **Llanfabon** (Gla, Gw); Pabo, as in **Llanbabo** (Môn); and Deiniol, as in **Llanddeiniol** (Dyf). Meirion not only had his church at **Llanfeirian** (Môn), but also gave his name to **Meirionnydd** (Gwy), the region. Others accorded saintly status were Edern, as in **Bodedern** (Môn), literally 'Dwelling (of) Edern' and Edeirnion, as in **Dyffryn Edeirnion** (Gwy) — *dyffryn*, 'vale'.

Illtud, mentioned above in connexion with two separate prehistoric sites, takes pride of place among the Armorican evangelists whose work bore fruit in Wales. His own most notable contribution was the monastic foundation at **Llanilltud Fawr** (Gla), which gained high repute as a spiritual fountainhead and seat of learning. (The alternative designation of the place, **Llantwit**, stems partly from the Irish version of the saint's name.)

According to one tradition, St David (Dewi Sant), one of the best known of the Welsh-born saints, was educated here before going on to found his own monastery, **Tyddewi** (Dyf), 'House (of) David'. (The site is of course also known as **Menevia**, which is a latinised form of Welsh **Mynwy**, from *Monowiā*.) St David's popularity is attested by the large number of **Llanddewi** names elsewhere in Wales.

Other important saints of native birth were Cadog, Beuno and Tysilio. Thus we find **Llangatwg** (Gla, Pow), **Llanfeuno** (He) —

anglicised **Llanveynoe** — and **Llandysilio** (Clw, Dyf, Gwy, Môn). Padarn, who is claimed by both Wales and Brittany independently, has likewise given his name to more than one locality, including **Llanbadarn Fynydd** (Pow), mentioned in Chapter 2.

From the course of the book generally, it will be clear that some ecclesiastical sites and other church-orientated places were named fairly explicitly, but without reference to particular individuals. Further examples to be added to this category include **Llan**, 'Church' with no addition (at least 28 cases throughout Wales), **Clas** (Gla), 'Church', 'Religious community', **Cydblwyf** (Dyf), 'Joint parish' (*plwyf*), **Hen Briordy** (Dyf), 'Old priory', **Rhandir Abad** (Dyf), 'Territory (of) abbot', **Abaty Cwm-hir** (Pow), 'Abbey (of) valley long', **Bwlch-y-person** (Dyf), 'Pass (of) the parson', and perhaps **Bryn Brawd** (Dyf), 'Hill (of) brother', i.e. 'friar' (*brawd* also signifies 'judgment').

It must be noted too that the use in place-names of terms such as *cum*, 'together with', *iuxta*, 'near', *supra*, 'above', *infra*, 'below' etc. is itself indicative of church influence, since it presupposes the existence of a literate clerical secretariat familiar with Latin. Indeed, from the 5th century to the 11th century and beyond, the recording of nearly *all* place-names, whether ecclesiastical or civil, will have been carried out by clerical scribes in the absence of a definable middle class and with much of the nobility unable (or unwilling) to read or write. Their industriousness in the service of church and state is amply demonstrated in Wales by (for example) the *Book of Llandaff* and in England — more impressively still — by *Domesday Book*.

Particularly interesting in an administrative context are the old commote names **Maelor Saesneg** (Pow) and **Maelor Gymraeg** (Pow) — 'Maelor Saxon' and 'Maelor Welsh' respectively (the precise meaning of *maelor* is uncertain). Here the overlapping of nationalities typical of most border areas is clearly mirrored, as is the necessity of making distinctions — compare **English Frankton** (Sa), **Welsh Frankton** (Sa), where the language of description is English. In the same context, the clerical influence just noted manifests itself in old forms such as *Haya Wallensis* (Pow), which is

49

a combination of Anglo-French *haie*, 'enclosure' (Old English *gehaeg*) and the Latin word signifying 'of the Welshmen'. The old names **Morton Anglicorum** (Clw) and **Morton Wallicorum** (Clw), which also draw the distinction between Englishmen and Welshmen, are other typical examples of what might — almost — be dubbed 'clerical hybrids'. **Rhiwsaeson** (Pow), 'Hill (of) Saxons' is of course purely Welsh.

Lay interests are to the forefront in **Tirybrenin** (Gla), 'Land (of) the king' and **Cyfoethybrenin** (Dyf), 'Possession (of) the king', as they are also in **Tremarchog** (Dyf), 'Hamlet (of) knight', and **Trefaldwyn** (Pow), 'Hamlet (of) Baldwin' — the name here referring to the Marcher lord Baldwin de Bollers, who was granted the place in 1102 by Henry I (its 'English' name **Montgomery** goes back to Earl Roger de Montgomery, who built the original castle here c. 1072). Baldwin's name appears to be echoed in nearby **Ffridd Faldwyn**, site of a hillfort. We also find **Cantref** (Pow), 'Hundred', as a simplex name, and formed on similar terse lines were the old commote and hamlet names **Perfedd** (Dyf), 'Middle', and **Swydd** (Pow), 'District'. At **Gwaunyterfyn** (Clw), 'Meadow (of) the boundary', the boundary in question may have been civil or ecclesiastical (or both), while the two worlds seem to meet in **Eglwys Cwmwdig** (Dyf), 'Church pertaining to commote'.

Finally, **Crug Gwyddel** (Pow), 'Mound (of) Irishman', **Gwernygwyddel** (Dyf), 'Alder-swamp (of) the Irishman', and **Gwyddelwern** (Gwy), 'Irishman's alder-swamp' could all testify to the influence of Brychan's family, and the same applies to **Llan y Gwydyll** (Môn), 'Church (of) the Irishmen'. **Castell Fflemish** (Dyf) stems direct from Flemish settlement, which, both here and elsewhere, was set in train by the Norman kings, beginning with Henry I; in western Wales, the Flemings were the pioneers of large-scale sheep-farming geared to the production of cloth.

Chapter 4

A Note on the Accent

Why is it that so many of even the most ordinary Welsh and English place-names tend, with the passage of time, to become increasingly subject to distortion or loss of meaning? This crucial question, touched on earlier but left temporarily in abeyance, is due to be tackled in the next chapter. Since, however, any attempt at answers will inevitably involve reference to the Welsh accent or stress (´), the immediate task must be to trace its history in relation to the Brythonic-based place-names of Wales.

The vast majority of Modern Welsh words consisting of more than one syllable — and this includes strict compounds $(fx, f^{l}x)$, which count as single words — are accented on the penultimate, or last-but-one; e.g. *bendigédig* ('blessed'), *hebógau* ('hawks'), *llýgad* ('eye'). This means, of course, that in strict compounds of two syllables — e.g. *gláswellt*, '(green) grass', *lláethdy*, 'milk house' — the accent will be borne by the qualifying elements f, f^{l}, as indicated.

But we must be on our guard against thinking that there is some sort of 'special relationship' between qualifiers as such and the accent. In the pair of examples just cited, the accent falls on *glás* and *lláeth-* simply because they constitute the penultimate syllables, *not* because they happen to be qualifiers. Just as in a strict compound word of *three* syllables — e.g. *bugéildy*, 'shepherd house' — the accent is seen to fall on the *second* syllable, this being the penultimate, there are strict compounds of *four* syllables — e.g. *uchelgýllid*, 'chief rent' (*cýllid*) — in which the accent falls on a syllable (the *third*) belonging not to the qualifier at all but to the principal term, x.

History shows, in fact, that the accent in strict compound words and place-names generally is independent of the grammatical or syntactic function of any element containing the syllable on which it falls; and the truth of this can be tested by tracing the development of Romano-British strict compound names which have themselves survived into Modern Welsh or for which there are clear Modern Welsh analogues.

In Brythonic, the accent fell where it does now, on the penultimate. Since the vast majority of strict compound names contained four syllables, the accent therefore fell mostly on the third syllable. Thus, taking three familiar and typical examples, *Moridúno(n)*, 'Sea fort', *Letocéto(n)*, 'Grey wood', and *Camboglánna*, 'Crooked bank' or 'At-the-bend bank' would all have been accented as indicated — i.e. on the first syllable of the principal term as opposed to the qualifier (and likewise **lactotígos*, 'milk house').

With the general loss of final syllables, c. 500-550, the accent became fixed on what had hitherto been the penultimate, but was now the ultimate, syllable. This new accent-position, surviving the subsequent changes affecting vowels and consonant-groups through the Primitive Welsh period, lasted until not later than c. 1100. By then, the Old Welsh forms of our three compound names were respectively *Merdín* (or *Mirdín*), *Luitcóit*, *Camlánn* (and likewise *laith-tí*), with the accent still on the principal term.

Around 1100, however, the accent shifted, coming to rest once more on the penultimate syllable — hence (in Modern Welsh spelling) *Mýrddin*, *Llwýtgoed*, *Cámlan* (and likewise *lláethdy*). The accent-shift itself may or may not have been due to a feeling that penultimate stress was more congenial to the language; but whatever the reasons, it seems clear that they cannot be tied to grammatical or syntactic function.

This important point might be further illustrated by looking at names like Romano-British *Crococalána*, probably 'Tumulus settlement', f^1x. In this particular instance there is no descendant (the place being identified with Brough Castle, in England), since natural development was cut short by Anglo-Saxon conquest. Nevertheless, a Welsh analogue — if one existed — would take the form **Cruc(c)álan*, with the accent on the first syllable of the principal term, not on the qualifier (**Cruc-*, from **Crouco-*).

By the same token, the accent falls on the equivalent syllable in

Gwynfýnydd (Pow), 'Fair mountain', **Hirfýnydd** (Gla), 'Long mountain', **Henéglwys** (Môn), 'Old church', **Henféddau** (Dyf), 'Old graves', **Henfýnyw** (Dyf), 'Old Mynyw' — all strict compound names, and all with the qualifier *un*accented.

Improper Compounds

Strict compound names, then, are combinations of two words accented as though they were single words. Turning to *xf*, *xf¹* improper compound names (or 'name-phrases', Chapter 2), these consist of separate words, accented separately.

Here, the main accent tends to fall on a syllable (often the only one) of the second or qualifying element — usually, as we have seen, an adjective or a dependent genitive. So we find **Maes-gwýn** (Dyf) 'Plain fair', **Pen-týrch** (Gla) 'Head (of) boar', and large numbers of others.

Even where this is the case, however, it seems difficult to tie the accent firmly to syntactic function. Many names of this type may originally have borne separate accents — Máes Gwýn (from a notional *Mágos Wíndos*), Pén Týrch (from a notional *Pénnon Tórcī*), the first element being weakened when the main accent became fixed on the ultimate, c. 500-550. Moreover, it is to be assumed that in names like **Llanddíngad** (Gw), 'Church (of) Dingad', **Llanédern** (Gla), 'Church (of) Edern', **Llandúdno** (Gwy), 'Church (of) Tudno', **Bryncélyn** (Clw), 'Hill (of) holly-trees' etc. the accent originally fell on the *ultimate* syllables of the second (qualifying) elements; but — as with Gwynfynydd etc. — it has since come to rest on the penultimate, the names being regarded as units, i.e. single words. That is, the accent rests on the penultimate *not* because this belongs to the qualifying element, but because the penultimate is its natural home.

We have already seen how an improper compound name can have its whole structure changed through the agency of the accent. In **Abermaw** (**Abermo**), the original qualifying element was the river-name, *Mawdd* — hence the meaning, 'Mouth (of) Mawdd'.

At the time of its coining in Primitive Welsh, and presumably for as long as it was perceived as having two distinct elements, the name was accented on the second (qualifying) element. The distinction grew blurred, however, and the name was seen as a single unit; as a result, it was accented *Abérmawdd*. With subsequent loss of -*dd*, and the replacement of initial *A*- by the definite article, the end-product in speech was *Y Bérmo*. Not only has the speech-accent deserted the qualifier for the principal term, but the name has also been severely distorted from the original in consequence.

Other names where the tendency to see improper compounds as units has attracted the stress from the qualifier to the principal term include **Brýngwyn** (Gw), 'Hill fair', **Mynýdd-mawr** (Gwy), 'Mountain great', **Tréfor** (Clw, Gwy), 'Hamlet great', **Mínffordd** (Gwy), 'Edge (of) road', **Péntir** (Gwy), 'Head or end (of) land', and **Pénmon** (Môn), 'Promontory (of) Môn'.

The last six examples are all taken from Sir John Morris Jones' *Welsh Grammar*, Sec. 46 ii (3). But perhaps more telling still are the seven that immediately follow in the same section of this great work. Each is an improper compound name containing the definite article, and in each case the accent (following the instinct towards the penultimate) has come to rest on the definite article itself — which is surely remarkable to say the least.

The names are **Pen-ý-berth** (Gwy) and **Pen-é-berth** (Dyf), both 'End (of) the hedge'; **Tal-ý-bryn** (Clw), 'Front (of) the hill'; **Clust-ý-blaidd** (Clw), 'Ear (of) the wolf'; **Moel-ý-ci** (Gwy), 'Hill (of) the dog'; **Llan-é-cil** = **Llanýcil** (Gwy), 'Church (of) the nook or recess'; and **Pen-é-goes** = **Penégoes** (Pow), literally 'End (of) the foot'. In three cases, as can be seen, the retention of the spelling *e* for the definite article *y* is a potential ingredient for further weakening of the sense.

It is probable that Welsh readers will know of other improper compound names where shifts of accent have taken place along lines similar to those outlined above. Meanwhile there appears to be little doubt that the pull of the accent itself is often a more potent factor in the development of given place-names than any conscious feeling that these names should make unequivocal sense; and since developments of an anomalous nature in which the accent plays a part are usually aided and abetted by certain other conditions, we now move on to see what these conditions may be — in English as well as in Welsh.

Chapter 5

Place Names and Language

'Os gwelwch fannod, *yr* neu *y*, o flaen enw lle, nid gwir enw priod yw, ond enw cyffredin wedi ei wneud yn arbennig. Ni ddywedwn byth *Y Llundain*, achos enw lle arbennig yw Llundain, ac nid oes angen bannod o'i flaen.'

— Sir Ifor Williams, *Enwau Lleoedd*

('If you see the definite article, *yr* or *y*, in front of a place-name, it is not a true proper noun, but a common noun, having been made special. We never say *The London*, because London is a special place-name, and there is no need of the definite article in front of it.')

What is said above regarding London encapsulates an important truth, but its ramifications are perhaps not immediately obvious. The task of the present chapter, therefore, will be to examine how names of the London type — taken as a general category — come to be regarded as 'special' (*arbennig*), and to trace the chief routes by which they arrive at their special status.

London itself, of course, Romano-British *Londinium*, happens to be a name of particularly obscure origin, but this fact is of no great consequence in the present context. There are hundreds of other names in England, of pure English origin, which are just as 'special' as London, and precisely by virtue of being regarded as proper nouns or names (*enwau priod*). Indeed, for this very reason, the development of some of these English names will shortly receive attention. Not only do they share certain things in common with their Welsh counterparts, but they also have a certain relevance to the matters dealt with in the next and last chapter.

However, let us begin by looking more closely at what happened to the two Welsh names *Abermawdd* and *Aberffrawf*. As early as Chapter 2, the shifting of the accent was cited as the chief cause leading to the distortion of both names; but — as made clear by the further remarks on Abermawdd in Chapter 4 — the effects of this shifting have really to be considered in conjunction with other factors, notably obsolescence (or obsoletism).

Indeed, it might be supposed that this factor alone suffices to explain most cases of distortion or loss of meaning. For if words used as place-name elements die out subsequently in ordinary language (a fate which, for a variety of unpredictable reasons, may befall almost any word in any period), why should they be expected to go on conveying their meaning in the restricted environment of the place-names?

Thus obsolescence undoubtedly played its part in the change of *Abermawdd* to **Abermo**. Here, the significance of the earlier *-mawdd* is not absolutely clear, this element being possibly the relic of a personal name. In any event it has left no descendant in Modern Welsh, so that (bearing in mind the Welsh tendency to drop final *-dd* in speech) the change to *-maw* and then *-mo* might very well have taken place even had the accent *not* shifted position. (In fact, original *mawdd* appears to have survived the shift, since — as we have seen — it led to English Bar*mouth*.)

Likewise, the obsolescence factor was operative in the change of *Aberffrawf* to **Aberffro**. For although, in this instance, *ffrawf* is traced back to **frām-*, with the probable meaning 'flood', there is again no direct descendant in Modern Welsh, and the meaning was already obscured by the dropping of organic *-f* (from *-m*). In turn, the loss of *-f* allowed the resultant *-ffraw* to be simplified to *-ffro*.

All this said, however, it is not quite so easy to explain the spoken forms *Y Bérmo* and *Y Bérffro*, in both of which the first element (*Aber-*) has also suffered mutilation. If *aber* itself had become obsolete in ordinary speech, the fact that both Abermo and Aberffro would then have consisted entirely of obsolete elements would make the accent-shift — seen as a mechanical process — easier to understand. But *aber*, in the senses 'estuary', 'confluence', remains a meaningful word to this day in Modern Welsh. It might, then, have been expected that the very geographical situation of the places (whence, of course, their names) would have helped *Aber-* to preserve its integrity as an element, resisting the pull of the accent. This, however, was not the case — even though a great many other *Aber-* elements survive unscathed.

(It is to be noted that Gerald of Wales, writing c. 1188 in his *Journey Through Wales*, shows himself fully conversant with at least one of the meanings of *aber*; for he makes a point of telling us, in Book 1, Chapter 2, that Aberhonddu is so called precisely because that is 'where the River *Hotheni* flows into the Usk.' There is perhaps no reason to suppose that he was ignorant of the meaning 'estuary'.)

Let us look at another Welsh example which poses similar problems. This is **Trefyclawdd** (Pow), 'Hamlet or town (of) the dyke' (English *Knighton*). Here, too, an xf^1 name came to be regarded as a single word, and was duly accented *Trefýclawdd*; loss of final *-dd* followed, the resulting *-claw* was simplified to *-clo*, and today **Trefyclo** is an accepted version of the earlier name.

Again, however, the question to be asked is — how did *clawdd*, 'dyke', 'embankment', which (like *aber*) is still a meaningful word in the Welsh language, manage to degenerate so easily into *clo*? Might it not have been expected that — at least as long as Welsh continued to be spoken in this area, so heavily influenced by English — the knowledge of the famous Offa's Dyke (whence the original Welsh name) would act as a 'semantic reminder' in respect of *clawdd*, militating against both loss of *-dd* and the pull of the accent? After all, 'Offa's Dyke' in Welsh is *Clawdd Offa*, unambiguously.

By contrast, the name Trefyclo is ambiguous as well as corrupt, for it so happens that there is a Welsh word *clo* which means 'lock'. It seems unlikely that this fact ever registered consciously with Welsh-speakers, the greater probability being that the name-element *-clo* came to rank as a semantically null particle. Nevertheless, the result is a tangled situation in which the written form Trefyclo might well, on the face of it, signify 'Hamlet or town (of) the lock', while the spoken form Trefyclo is — owing to the accent-position — all but incomprehensible.

A Sub-class

Taken separately or together, obsolescence and the effects of the Welsh accent-shift serve to bring out the important point that meaning is not felt to be a necessary property of any given place-name, no matter how freely it continues to be used in the wider framework of ordinary speech. Looked at objectively, this fact may strike us as somewhat surprising, since there must presumably have been a time when all place-names had meanings which were quite clear to the communities by whom or for whom they were designed. Indeed, the downgrading of meaning suggests that place-names ought to be seen as constituting a sub-class within the living language — regardless, in the present frame of reference, of whether the language concerned is Welsh or English.

(It is true that 'popular etymology' or 're-interpretation' sometimes takes a hand in an attempt to make names less alien or uncongenial — one good example here being Barmouth, from *Y Bérmawdd* or a form approximating to it. But cases where such rationalised versions actually succeed in becoming established are not all that frequent, compared with the vast numbers of meaningless names left unrationalised.)

Since the primary concern in this chapter is meaning (or rather the loss of it) in place-names generally, it seems legitimate to find out what can be learned from English names. Here the accent, which with few exceptions in Old English rested solidly on the first syllable, plays only a minor rôle. But because case-endings were lost at a much later date in English than in Welsh, and because the supply of early forms is much more plentiful in England than in Wales, the factors contributing to loss of meaning can be pinned down with greater clarity. In certain cases, too, broad parallels can be drawn between English and Welsh names — though they must not, of course, be stretched too far.

The obsolescence factor is seen at work in both simplex and double-element names. **Ower** (Ha), for example, spelt *Ore* in 1284, derives from Old English *ōra*, 'shore', 'bank', and the 1284 form shows the appropriate Middle English development of this word; it did not, however, survive in ordinary speech, and this fact alone would account for the present name, which is not only meaningless but also phonologically 'wrong' (we might have expected *Ore, *Oore, *Oare, or even *Awre). A suitable Welsh parallel here might be the river name **Gele** (Clw), which goes back to an original *gelau*, 'sword-blade', 'spear-point'; had this word not become obsolete, the change *-au* to *-e* might conceivably not have occurred.

Galton (Do) was spelt *Gaveltone* in 1086, the first element representing Old English *gafol*, 'tax', 'rent' — a word which (except in the legal term *gavelkind*) also failed to survive. We can say, then, that the fact that *gafol* became obsolete is sufficient explanation for its corruption to *Gal-* in this particular name; while its appearance intact in **Gavelacre** (Ha) does not, of course, render it any more *meaningful*. It is interesting, too, that a form *Galtone* was also recorded for Galton in 1086, alongside the correct form — indicating, perhaps, that the name had already lost its meaning by that date. (Later forms seem to show association with Middle English *gaule*, 'bog-myrtle', so that Galton may also provide an example of popular etymology.) Meanwhile it is probably the strength of the accent on the first syllable which has reduced original *-tūn* to *-ton*, i.e. preventing its full development to *-town*.

English names like Ower and Galton, then, correspond to Welsh names like Gele and Abermo in so far as their corruption, as well as their loss of meaning, can be sufficiently explained in terms of obsolescence. They should, however, be distinguished from names — also meaningless today — containing one or more words as elements which, although indeed obsolete, have not been subject to serious corruption. Phonologically, these names have developed more or less as though the word(s) comprising them had continued in general use.

Thus **Loose** (K) is the expected Modern English result of Old English *hlōse*, 'shelter', 'pigsty', from which it ultimately derives; but this word survived only in dialect, so that to the vast majority of people nowadays Loose would convey only a false sense or no sense at all. With it may be compared — for example — Welsh **Powys**, which (as already mentioned) probably stems from a Latin *pāgē(n)ses*, 'province-dwellers', 'district-dwellers'; the phonological development is impeccable, even though the meaning must have been lost at a much earlier date than with *hlōse*.

Among double-element names of the same type are English **Wonersh** (Sr), reflecting Old English (*aet*) *wōgan ersce*, '(at the) crooked field' (both the original elements being quite obsolete), and Welsh **Myrddin**, later **Caerfyrddin**, whose development is exactly what would be expected — even though its 'etymon' (*Moridūnon*, 'Sea-fort', Chapter 2) left no meaningful descendant in Modern Welsh. In that they are all, today, empty of meaning, Loose, Powys, Wonersh and Caerfyrddin exhibit what might be termed 'shadow-etymologies'.

Now while it can be readily understood that corruptions are very likely to follow (and loss of meaning is almost certain to follow) on the heels of obsolescence, these 'shadow-etymologies' nevertheless raise an interesting question. Superficially, they are no different from names like — say — **Hawkridge** (Brk) and **Llwytgoed** (Gla). With the first of these, the recorded form of 956, *Heafochrycg* (Old English *heafoc*, 'hawk', plus *hrycg*, 'ridge') shows that the constituent elements of the name developed just as they have (as words) in ordinary speech; in short, Hawkridge still actually *means* 'hawk ridge'. Likewise with Llwytgoed; here, although we have no evidence that the name goes back as far as a Brythonic *Lētocēton*, 'Grey wood' (it may have been coined later), the *meaning* is not in dispute.

The question is, then: Why do so many place-names containing elements which have developed normally and retained their meaning in ordinary speech fail to conform to the pattern of Hawkridge and Llwytgoed? The problem is a complex one, and far from easy to grapple with. But — leaving Llwytgoed aside for the present — the evidence of English names clearly shows that the Hawkridge's are in a minority; and it is possible to isolate at least some of the reasons underlying this state of affairs.

Location-markers

First, we need to be clear about the 'case-endings' referred to earlier. Suffice it to say that Old English was a fully-inflected language; that is, the generality of words took prescribed endings according to their function within sentences. Such endings when added to nouns, adjectives and the definite article (which alone concern us here) are known as case-endings. They were — so to speak — invariables designed to cope with an enormous range of contextual variations. However, as the language progressed it evolved new mechanisms for performing this task; Middle English (c. 1100-1500) saw the gradual decay of the case-system up to the point where it virtually ceased to exist.

In Old English, place-names were inflected in context like any other words (or combinations of words); indeed, large numbers of names are first encountered in inflected forms from which their uninflected nominatives have to be deduced. This process is not for the most part unduly difficult, but it may well be a little misleading. For we cannot always be sure that a name did not, in fact, originate *within* a given context — its function there being literally that of 'location-marker'. To assume that an uninflected Old English nominative — i.e. what is understood as a 'formal place-name' — pre-dated the inflected word or phrase first recorded may, in some cases, be to put the cart before the horse.

Certain names in England still retain traces of the inflected definite article, and were clearly designed to act as location-markers. Thus **Noke** (O), spelt *Ac(h)*am in 1086, *Ake* in the early 13th century, is the relic of Old English (*aet*) *thāem ācum*, '(at) the oaks' — showing the plural of the dative as required by the preposition *aet*; in Middle English, the phrase took the form (*atten*) *oke(n)* — but the final -*n* of *atten* was then wrongly attached to *oke(n)* itself, whence ultimately Noke. It is interesting that the modern name seems to represent fossilisation in speech of a case-ending (-*n*) which is disregarded in the early written forms. If there is a queer logic here, it has nevertheless defeated its own object, since to modern ears and eyes Noke is meaningless.

A few other place-names in English survive (usually, though not always, involving natural features) in which the definite article was specifically used in order to isolate and define given spots in relation to their surroundings. It was used for the same purpose in Welsh names, too — as, indeed, is pointed out by Sir Ifor Williams himself. A little further on in the passage quoted at the head of this chapter, as a corollary to his remarks on London, he adds the following:

'Ond cymerer enw cyffredin fel craig: i nodi craig arbennig rhaid i ni ddweud *Y Graig* . . .'

('But take a common noun like rock: to denote a special rock we have to say *The Rock* . . .')

Names of the Noke type, then are of intrinsic interest in that they retain traces of the Old English definite article, whose overt use in place-names is rare. (A Welsh example of confusion between definite article and principal term is **Rhewl**, occurring three times in Clwyd, the -*r* of original *Yr Heol*, 'The road' having been carried forward.) At the same time, however, they serve to illustrate the peculiar effects likely to result in English place-names from the perpetuation of outdated case-endings or from other forms of fossilisation; and it will repay us to look at a cross-section of other names in which the definite article is not involved.

Each (K), *Ece* 1086, has developed from the mutated dative singular (*ēce*) of Old English *āc*, 'oak'; while **Acomb** (Nb, YN, YW) is shown by early spellings to go back to the unmutated dative plural (*ācum*). The second of these two names is effectively fossilised, the first owes its modern form directly to an inflected — hence outdated — word. In both instances, too, it is the locative (or 'locational') sense that is unconsciously retained; that is, neither name has been reduced to its simple nominative, 'Oaks' (= Middle English *ōkes*). Meaninglessness is the result in terms of Modern English.

By contrast, **Occold** (Sf) has sprung from the Old English

63

nominative *ācholt*, 'oak copse', which counts grammatically as a proper compound. The name was spelt *Ocolt* in 1254, at which time the original sense of the compound may still have been remembered — Middle English *ōk*, 'oak' plus *holt*, 'copse'. Nevertheless, the Modern English spelling and pronunciation show that the vowel of the first element in the place-name compound was shortened (*ōk->occ-*), whereas in ordinary speech its long value was retained (*ōk* > *oak*). The reason may have been that the sense of the whole compound used to form the place-name was finally lost, *ōk* then being shortened by analogy with other Middle English vowel-shortenings in ordinary speech — e.g. *fōdor* > *fodder*, 'fodder', *blǣedre* > *bladder*, 'bladder' etc. — which did not, of course, involve loss of *meaning*. At all events, modern Occold is itself meaningless, in spite of the fact that both its constituent elements survive as meaningful words in everyday language (if one may stretch a point with *holt*).

Let us now look at what may be called 'pseudo-compounds'. By this term is meant any English place-name which originated not as an Old English proper compound (in which only the second element was inflected) but as a combination of separate words, separately inflected. The combination might consist of adjective-plus-noun or of noun-plus-noun; if the first, the adjective is almost invariably found in its 'weak' form — the form used attributively after the definite article and having precisely the function of making definite or particular associated with it. (In Old English charters, for example, phrases such as *on clofenan hlinc*, 'at cloven hill', *tō scearpan aecge*, 'to sharp edge-of-hill' etc. show the adjective in its weak form, with a preceding 'the' implied.)

Thus **Naunton** (G1), near Winchcombe, is referred to contextually in a will of 1004 in the phrase *aet Niwantune*, 'at (the) new *tūn*', showing both adjective and noun in the inflected (dative) form after *aet* (adjectives and nouns agree grammatically in Old English). The nominative sense — 'New *tūn*' — will presumably have been quite clear to local Anglo-Saxons, familiar with the precise significance of *tūn*; indeed, the very nature of the name argues for its meaningfulness.

Now although the (West Saxon) spelling of 1004 does not reflect the fact, the weak adjectival *Niwan-* goes back to an original Anglian *nēowan* (nominative *nēowa*), giving a later West Midland *nōwen*, whence *Naun-*. But this inflected dialectal form must have lost its import (i.e. as a dative, following *aet*) once the case-system had broken down; persistence with it has resulted in a meaningless name. (The 1086 form, *Niwetone*, would probably have given a modern **Newton* — or perhaps even **Newtown*, with both elements fully developed.)

There are even cases where — either in error or through scribal idiosyncrasy — *aet* is treated as in integral part of place-names. Thus, in an early reference to the present **Salisbury** (W), the annal for 552 in the *Anglo-Saxon Chronicle* (A text) states that in this year Cynric fought against the Britons at the place *'the is genemned aet Searo byrg'* ("which is called 'at *Searo byrg*' ") — where *byrg* is nevertheless in the dative case as if part of a prepositional phrase. In the E text *aet* does not appear (and it was later crossed out in the A text), but the name is still given as *Searo byrig*, with *byrig* in the dative case; only the B and C texts show the nominative form *Searo burh*, as the sense requires. Similar incorporation of *aet* into the structure of names is also found in Anglo-Saxon charters.

(This mistreatment of names whose original background was locational or directional is not limited to Anglo-Saxon England. The name **Istanbul** or **Stamboul**, for example, arose from the Greek phrase *eis tèn pólin*, meaning 'to the town'; and it is possible that more than one Romano-British name was fossilised in an inflected form whose original import had been forgotten — see Chapter 6.)

Turning to the noun-plus-noun type of name, a good example here is **Gatton** (Sr). The place features in a will of c. 971-88, the reference being to a bequest of land *'on Gata-tune'*, literally 'in of-goats *tūn*', showing the genitive plural of *gāt*, 'goat' and the dative singular of *tūn* (as required by the preposition *on*). Again, it would appear that the sense must once have been quite unambiguous. Nevertheless, at some point in late Old English the vowel of *Gāt-* was shortened to *Gat-*; final *-a* was reduced to *-e*

65

(*Gatetuna* 1121), and then lost, hence Gatton. Similar vowel-shortening took place in **Gatacre** (Sa), **Gatcombe** (So) and in one or two other names, whereas in **Goathurst** (So), spelt *Gothurste* in 1292, *gāt* is seen following its ordinary-speech development, as it is also in **Goathill** (Do), *Gothull* 1254-56. (As is usual, *-tūn* has been shortened to *-ton*, instead of yielding *-town*, which is the correct outcome in ordinary speech.)

Audio-visual Signs

In the examples discussed above (all of which, whatever the particular circumstances surrounding their origins, are established place-names), meaning has been lost or severely damaged. But we still need to bear in mind, not only the many place-names referred to in charters and other sources whose sites have not been identified, but also location-marking phrases such as *on clofenan hlinc*, *tō scearpan aecge* etc., which themselves deserve tō be seen as potential place-name material.

Who would care to wager on how *tē scearpan aecge* might have developed, for instance, had social, economic or legal factors decreed that it should become a 'formal place-name'? A nominative **Sharpedge* would be logical, of course; but, as we have seen, logic by no means always decides the issue. A 'false' nominative **Sharpenidge* might be just as likely: compare **Bradnidge** (Bk), where the final *-n* of an inflected *brādan*, 'broad' (or of an inflected personal name, **Brāda*) has been retained to this day, with shortening and fossilisation of *-ā-* and corruption of *ecg* (= *aecg*).

And what about *on clofenan hlinc*? Old English *(ge)clofen*, 'cloven', 'split' gave Modern English *cloven* (still, of course, meaningful), while *hlinc* survived in dialect as *lynch*, 'ridge', 'hillside'; a nominative **Clovenlynch*, then, seems logical enough. But contrast **Clannaborough** (D), *Cloueneberge* 1239; here the original meaning was indeed 'Cloven hillside', but both elements have been corrupted and the sense of the first element is totally obscured in the modern name.

This is not to say, of course, that logical developments are non-existent (we have already noted Hawkridge, if only as an exception), or that no contextual phrases would have developed logically had the opportunity to develop come their way in the first place. In general terms, however, it may be argued that location-markers, once they have gained currency in that fixed capacity, show a strong tendency to change their status from that of meaningful descriptive phrases or common nouns (*enwau cyffredin*), often in compound form, to that of proper nouns (*enwau priod*), with meaning now accorded very low priority. More often than not they develop along lines tangential to those of ordinary speech; sooner or later, indeed, large numbers of them come to act as mere audio-visual signs.

It is true that certain words (in Welsh as well as English) must have had special meanings in the place-naming context which set them apart from their ordinary-speech counterparts and which encouraged their fossilisation within that context; for example, Old English -*hām*-, 'homestead', 'village' etc. is invariably fossilised in place-names (with shortened -*a*-, -*ham*-), instead of developing to Middle English *hōm*, Modern English *home*, 'home'. It is true, too, that words used as elements in compounds often lose the semantic force attaching to them as independent speech-units: the constituent parts of *homestead* are not quite the same as either *home* or *stead* when used separately.

But although these facts may go some way towards explaining loss of meaning (especially in names whose constituent elements are not obsolete in the strict sense), they do not really explain the widespread tolerance of such loss. In everyday practice, most of us are quite content with our audio-visual signs — just as, perhaps less contentedly, we go along with the postcode.

These remarks apply more particularly to names in England, where (as stated) the supporting evidence is more copious. But with all due deference to Sir Ifor Williams, the phenomenon of status-change is observable in Wales also. As Sir Ifor points out, in order to pluck a given rock from anonymity it is necessary to prefix the definite article (or to use an adjective or a personal name); so *craig* becomes *Y Graig*. However, once the purpose of definition has been achieved, it is very common for the defining word to be dropped again: witness all those Welsh names in which a lenited initial letter is the sole indicator of its former presence, and those cases where — as in **Efenechdyd** (Clw), for **Y Fenechdid**, 'The monk house' — it has been mistakenly incorporated into the principal term.

Measured in terms of prestige, the difference between a name like London and a name like Efenechdyd could hardly be greater. Nevertheless, as a result of changing status from that of meaningful expression to that of meaningless proper name, they rank as equals on the semantic scale. Both, effectively, can be described as audio-visual signs; and there is no firm guarantee that **Graig** (Clw, Pow), 'Rock' may not — one day — come to merit the same description.

Chapter 6

The Brythonic Factor in England

'When we remember the close connections between Gaul and Britain and that schools existed in Britain at which Druids from the Continent acquired a higher learning, we may accept the probability that the British language could be, and was, written and read.'

— S. Frere, *Britannia* (1978), pp. 350-51

'Perhaps, in some minor ecclesiastical library, lurking anonymously behind the spine of a manuscript labelled *Tractatus* or *Leges*, there is pristine copy of a *Notitia Britanniarum*, protected by a layer of dust that began in the 5th century.'

— A.L.F. Rivet and Colin Smith, *The Place-Names of Roman Britain* (1981), p. 10

Having looked at some of the ways in which place-names were constructed in Old English, and having duly noted some of their peculiar features, we are now better placed to see how names of known Romano-British origin were 'taken over' by the Anglo-Saxons and fitted into this same Old English tongue.

The method adopted here will be, first, to give examples of the principal ways in which the business was handled, and, secondly, to discuss some of the difficulties surrounding what is a complex and by no means uncontroversial subject. It may well be that the nature of these difficulties is unfamiliar to the majority of readers, since the amount of easily accessible literature concerning them is still far from extensive.

Not least for this reason, brief mention must be made of the sources from which modern knowledge of the place-names of Roman Britain is chiefly derived. They range in time from the Greek Herodotus, writing in the 5th century BC, to the English Bede, whose famous *Ecclesiastical History* (first written in Latin) dates from c. 730 AD; and they include not only the works of many other individual writers using Latin or Greek (here belongs the *Geography* of Ptolemy, c. 150 AD) but also certain official or semi-official documents relating directly to the Roman Empire. Most important among these are the so-called *Antonine Itinerary* (road-books), spanning the early 1st to the late 3rd centuries AD, and the *Notitia Dignitatum* (a kind of bureaucratic survey), collated c. 395-408 AD. The *Ravenna Cosmography* (a list of place-names with supplementary text), is thought to have been compiled c. 700 AD by a single cleric from the town referred to in the work's title, and contains many inaccuracies.

Anglo-Brythonic

As already indicated, those recorded place-names of Roman Britain known as *Romano-British* are essentially Brythonic rather than Latin. It was some of these names, plus others taken to be Brythonic but not actually recorded by the Romans, that were adapted at various dates by the Anglo-Saxon settlers; and it seems legitimate to regard the resulting forms as *Anglo-Brythonic* creations.

These creations show varying degrees of resemblance to the originals — which, it must be remembered, will usually (if perhaps not always, see below) have developed in Brythonic speech beyond the stages exhibited in the written forms. In addition, some of the written forms themselves may not exactly mirror those current in everyday usage. They present the same kind of problem as was seen with e.g. Naunton in the last chapter, where the contextual (inflected) form, with -n, has ousted what (by late Middle English times at least) would have been the more logical nominative

Nowton, *Newton* etc. However, this problem and others like it can be left aside until we have looked at the main types of Anglo-Brythonic name as they have actually been handed down to us.

(1) The first type is exemplified by **Dover** (K). Here there seems to have been an attempt to give a literal or near-literal copy of the original, without addition or subtraction. The earliest known form in Old English, *Dofras*, dates from 696-716 and represents a Romano-British *Dubrā(s)*, 'Waters'; this, by the time the Anglo-Saxons are supposed to have taken it over (c. 475-500) would have developed to **Dofr(as)* in Late Brythonic (and would have given a Modern Welsh **Dofr*). Whether or not the Anglo-Saxons understood that the original name was a plural nominative, the fact is that their own Old English version happens to take that form.

Another name apparently taken over on the same principle was **Lympne** (K). This stems from Romano-British *Portus Lemanis*, which represents a fossilised Latin locative plural possibly taken from a Late Brythonic nominative plural **Limanis*. The earliest Old English form, 805-10, is (*of*) *Liminum*, itself a dative plural from which a nominative plural **Liminas* is inferrable. Again, then, the Anglo-Saxon version appears to echo the Late Brythonic fairly closely. (The -*p*- in the modern name is not organic.) The original Romano-British name derives from **lēm-*, 'elm' (Modern Welsh *llwyf*) or **līm-*, 'flood' (Modern Welsh *llif*), and the take-over will also have occurred at an early date — how early, we shall consider in due course.

(2) In the second type the Late Brythonic form — represented with a greater or lesser degree of accuracy — has had a purely Old English word added to it. By far the most common one is *ceaster* (Anglian *caester*), 'fortified place', 'city'; itself a borrowing from Latin (*castra*), it is usually found in conjuncton with the names of places known to have been cities or strongholds in Roman times — even where this fact is not indicated in the original names.

A typical example here is **Gloucester** (G1), a military site from the 1st century onwards. Listed as *Clevo* (for *Glevo*) in the *Antonine*

Itinerary and probably deriving from *Glēwon, 'Bright', the name was spelt (ad) Gleawece(a)stre in 804, showing the process of addition quite clearly. More frequently, however, *ceaster* was used to replace Romano-British -*duro*- and -*dunum*, 'fort' and 'hill-fort' respectively, indicating that the Anglo-Saxons understood their general sense. Addition of Old English *burh* in this context is not well attested, although it is sometimes used on its own to denote a known Roman fort, as with **Burgh Castle** (Sf), *Burch* 1086, Romano-British *Gariannum*.

Other words added in a descriptive or explanatory capacity include *feld*, 'open country', as in **Lichfield** (St), *Lyccidfelth*, *Liccidfeld* c. 730 (Latin Bede). Here the Old English word was added to the Primitive Welsh descendant of Romano-British *Letocetum* (*Lētocēton), already encountered. In the case of *Anderitos* — for *Anderitu or *Anderita, 'Great ford(s)' — the Romano-British name originally denoted the fort at modern **Pevensey** (Sx), but seems to have acquired a more extended meaning; thus the form *Andredesleage* in the annal for 477 in the *Anglo-Saxon Chronicle* shows the dative of Old English *lēah*, 'woodland', while in 1018 we find *Andredes Weald*, also 'Woodland of Andred' — i.e. the Sussex Weald.

The genitive of Old English *ware*, 'dwellers', 'inhabitants', was added to *Canti- (from Romano-British *Cantium*) to give the form *Cantwaraburg* of 754, 'Fort of the inhabitants of *Cant(i)*', (i.e. **Kent**), which led to modern **Canterbury** (K). In similar fashion, *scīr*, 'shire' was added (late) to Old English *Defna(s)*, which — like the Modern Welsh *Dyfnain(t)* — stems ultimately from Romano-British *Dumnonii*. As we have already seen, this term originally denoted the inhabitants of both modern Devon and Cornwall (and perhaps of parts of Somerset); at all events, the name Devon itself owes its present form to the Old English *Defnas*, *Defenas* just mentioned.

(3) In certain instances an original form was truncated before an Old English word was added. Here belong **Lanchester** (Du) and **Mancetter** (Wa). The first of these places was recorded c. 400 as *Longovicio*, interpreted to mean 'Place of the *Longovices'

(probably 'Ship-fighters'); by 1196 we find that the original second element (-*vicio*) has disappeared — having been replaced by Old English *ceaster* — while the full form of the new name, *Langecestr*', seems to show that Primitive Welsh **long*, 'ship' (from *longā*) has been confused with Old/Middle English *lang/long*, 'long'. Likewise the second element (*essedo*) of original *Manduessedo*, 'Horse-chariot', was dropped and *ceaster* added to the stump — which, in Primitive Welsh, would have given **Mann-*, with *-nd-* > *-nn-*. Hence the *Manacestre* of 1136, later Mancetter.

(4) In still other cases the first element of a Romano-British name appears to have been replaced by an Old English near-homophone with (not surprisingly) a totally different meaning. Thus the name *Sorviodunum* was apparently taken over when the first element, **Sorvio-* (meaning unknown) had reached the Primitive Welsh stage **Serw*; for this was substituted Old English *searu*, 'armour' (or maybe 'ruse', 'stratagem'), with *-dunum* (Primitive Welsh *-ddīn*) being translated (?) by *burh*. As we saw in Chapter 5, the *Anglo-Saxon Chronicle* records the form (*aet*) *Searo byrig* in the annal for 552 — Anglo-Norman influence being responsible for the change of *-r-* to *-l-* in modern Salisbury.

The name **York** has a not dissimilar history, though here both Romano-British elements were affected. The structure and meaning of the original *Eburacum* (**Eburācon*) were discussed in Chapter 2. By the time the Anglo-Saxons are thought to have encountered this name (late 5th century), the first element will have developed to **Evor-*, with lenition of *-b-* to *-v-*, and the second to *-ōg*; these two elements were assimilated to Old English *efor*, *eofor*, 'boar' and *wīc*, 'town' respectively, giving the *Eoforwicceaster* of the *Anglo-Saxon Chronicle* (644). The 'explanatory' *-ceaster* was subsequently dropped, the modern name resulting from the Scandinavian version (*Iorvík*) of *Eoforwic*.

(5) Lastly, Old English case-endings were not infrequently added to elements whose Brythonic origin is either known or inferred. This feature will be mentioned again later; instances involving an attested Romano-British name are provided by the Old English forms of *Isca Dumnoniorum*, modern **Exeter**. Here the

final -*n* associated with the oblique cases of weak adjectives and nouns is found on more than one occasion in the *Anglo-Saxon Chronicle* — e.g. *into Escan ceaster*, 876, 877 ('into Exeter', 'to Exeter'), where *Escan* represents original *Isca* ('**Exe**') + -*n*. (Here it seems likely that the force is genitival ('of Exe') rather than adjectival.) The latinised form *Ad-Escanceastre* of c. 750, showing *ad*, 'at' incorporated into the place-name, is also to be noted.

These, then, are the five principal ways in which Romano-British names were taken over by the Anglo-Saxon settlers. Whether or not one uses the term 'hybrid' to describe the names exemplified under headings (2), (3) and (5) would appear to be a matter of personal preference; certainly their modern forms contain elements derived from two different languages, so it might be somewhat pedantic to deny their hybrid character. As for 'tautological hybrids' like **Breedon** (Le), *Briudun* c. 730, *Breodun* c. 990, whose Old English second element *dūn*, 'down', 'hill' consciously or unconsciously translates the Primitive Welsh first element *bre- (from *brigā), examples are hard to come by among names with recorded Romano-British forms; but they will feature again shortly, as we move on to consider those names for which Brythonic origins can be postulated with varying degrees of certainty, but not absolutely proved.

Natural Selection

Some places whose Romano-British names are known to us still await identification on the map. In other instances, both names and places are known, but the names themselves — unlike those discussed above — were displaced rather than adapted by the Germanic settlers, thus leaving no descendants. Solutions as regards meaning have been suggested for most of the names falling into these two categories, but they are not really relevant here.

Nor can we go into the general question as to why some Romano-British names, rather than others, should have survived the test — in linguistic terms — of natural selection. This said, however, it is clear that most of those that *did* survive it denoted places ranking well up in the Roman scheme of things during their occupation — forts, cities, towns, *coloniae* (settlements for legionary veterans) and so on, all linked by the formidable network of Roman roads. Granted that a proportion of them must earlier have had their own importance in British eyes, such places were perhaps always likely to emerge from the upheavals of the 5th, 6th and 7th centuries as contenders for leading rôles on the political and/or religious stage; for the instinct towards historical continuity is a factor almost as potent as the practical considerations by which that continuity is ultimately determined. Moreover, Augustine's mission to England in 597 will have been nothing loth to build on the Roman past. It is surely no accident that Canterbury, Exeter, Gloucester, Lichfield, Lincoln, London, Rochester, Salisbury, Winchester and York — all places of prominence in Roman Britain — later acquired the status of English bishoprics.

At any rate, no real doubt surrounds the Brythonic origin of names in England for which Romano-British forms survive. Where such names were taken over by the Anglo-Saxons, invaluable opportunities exist for scholars — in both the Old English and Celtic fields — to observe what happened to them as a result. But the situation is somewhat different where comparably early forms are lacking. Here, the linguistic criterion is that of probability rather than certainty; if a name cannot be satisfactorily explained using the resources of Old English or Old Norse, then the most reasonable hypothesis is that it may be partly or wholly Brythonic (no consideration is given here to possible pre-Celtic or 'Old European' influences). However, in order to make good this hypothesis, proper account must be taken of the sound-changes known to have taken place in Late Brythonic and Primitive Welsh, and of how these changes are (or are not) reflected in the forms of the name recorded in English sources. What follows here is an attempt to deal with this complex subject as simply and accurately as possible, and to draw attention to one or two outstanding problems.

As early as the 19th century, it was recognised that numerous Celtic terms — mostly topographical, or picked out as occurring in topographical contexts — lay buried among the place-namings of England. One writer deserving special mention here is Isaac Taylor, whose *Words and Places* (1864) canvasses a wide range of such terms, the bulk of which are identified by Taylor as 'Cymric' — i.e. Brythonic — and some of which are now common currency in works on the subject (others, rightly, would be discountenanced). Handicapped by the relatively undeveloped state of philological knowledge in his day, Taylor nevertheless makes several important observations — pointing out, for example, that nearly all the larger rivers, as well as many mountains, hills and woods, bear names with Celtic bases. On a slightly different tack — but well in advance of his time — he also concludes on the evidence of place-name distribution that peaceful co-existence was the rule, rather than the exception, as regards the conquered British and the conquering Anglo-Saxons. (Some 15 years later, the historian E.A. Freeman is still thinking along the lines of 'extermination' and 'total displacement'.[*])

However, the first full-length study in English to tackle a specific aspect of the subject on a reasoned linguistic basis was Eilert Ekwall's *English River Names*, which did not appear until 1928. Four years earlier, in an essay contributed to Volume 1 of the publications of the English Place-Name Society, Ekwall had already emphasised the importance of 'The Celtic Survival' — this being the title of the essay, which makes a number of valuable points about the geographical distribution of Celtic names (including Brythonic ones) generally. Some of these points were taken up later by Kenneth Jackson (see below); but in Ekwall's eyes, all his own work prior to 1928 had really been a preparation for *River Names* itself (as he makes clear in the Introduction to this great work).

[*] 'England', in *Encyclopaedia Britannica*, 9th edition Vol. VIII, 1879

What concerns us particularly here is Ekwall's method of approach in *River Names*. It is essentially extrapolative, in that for the most part Ekwall was reasoning from the known to the unknown. Faced with a mass of non-Germanic names for which no Romano-British forms existed but which he took to be Brythonic, he set out to explain their existing forms in terms of what he called 'British sound history' — a subject he had studied for this specific purpose (Introduction, p. xxxv). At the same time, he had to take account of certain Old English sound-changes (such as *i*-umlaut) which to some extent overlap with Primitive Welsh ones.

A good illustration of the method is provided by Ekwall's solution of the river name **Glen** (Nb), *Gleni* c. 730, *Glene* c. 890. No word of Germanic origin is known which would explain this name, while Brythonic **glend-*, Primitive Welsh **glinn*, 'valley' (Modern Welsh *glyn*) would hardly be suitable. Ekwall therefore postulates an original Brythonic **Glanio-* or *Glaniā*, referred to **glano-*, 'clean', 'holy', 'beautiful' (Modern Welsh *glân*), giving the sense 'Clean (one)' etc. Not only is this sense appropriate, but the change of *-a-* to *-e-* is satisfactorily accounted for by final *i*-affection; this would have occurred in Late Brythonic c. 500 — before the Anglo-Saxons encountered the name (c. 550, see below), and also well before the time when Old English *i*-umlaut could have effected the same change independently.

As will be readily understood, a single example is inadequate to convey more than a fraction of the complexities involved; Ekwall is dealing not only with a wide range of names, but also with a wide range of sound-changes spread over a long period. Nevertheless, it suffices to provide an insight into the nature and value of the extrapolative method. In effect — and remembering that he envisages a background of inexorable, if uneven, Anglo-Saxon progress northwards and westwards — what Ekwall is saying in any given case is this: 'Here we have a Brythonic-based name; by the time the Anglo-Saxons adopted it — whenever that was — the sound-changes that can be shown to have occurred or not to have occurred in Late Brythonic or Primitive Welsh are such-and-such'. (The need to take due account of Old English sound-changes has already been noted.)

Problems of Dating

It can be seen that, provided Ekwall's initial premise concerning the Brythonic origin of given names is granted as correct, the rest of his method is quite valid; indeed it is a necessary method, and there is no doubting the masterly fashion in which he deploys it. However, what is lacking in the work as a whole is a solid chronological framework — whether we visualise this primarily in terms of sound-changes or in terms of Anglo-Saxon arrivals at this or that place. In fine, there is no tangible way in which the one set of data can be precisely correlated with the other. (This is simply an observation, and is not intended as criticism of a great achievement.)

The nature of the problem was firmly grasped by Kenneth Jackson, whose *Language and History in Early Britain* (1953) constitutes a major landmark in the study of Brythonic-based place-names in England. Strictly speaking, the latter were not Professor Jackson's primary concern; as the sub-title and his own prefatory remarks make clear, his overall purpose was to write a 'chronological history' of sound-changes in the Brythonic language and its descendants from the 1st century to the 12th, and the wealth of information provided in the course of this undertaking is extremely valuable for any number of different reasons.

Nevertheless, the most crucial sound-changes — i.e. those involving the transition from Late Brythonic to Primitive Welsh, Cornish and Breton — are all assigned by Jackson to the period c. 450-600, which coincides with much of the Anglo-Saxon settlement (others again belong to the 7th century). Jackson works out the sequence of these changes chiefly on the basis of internal linguistic evidence. However, in looking to fix on rather more precise individual datings, he places considerable weight on the external evidence afforded by Old English versions of Brythonic-based names (the relevance here, of course, being to Primitive Welsh and Cornish). 'The fact is' — Jackson asserts in his Preface — 'that little can be done unless the evidence of English place-names is thoroughly scrutinised.'

While acknowledging that a few important names like London, Kent and Thames may have been known to the Anglo-Saxons in advance, Jackson regards it as obvious (pp. 196-97) that they must in general have taken over given names when they first reached the places in question. Hence, if rough dates can be established for their arrival in any particular area, the forms of the names borrowed there will help us to determine whether this or that sound-change had or had not occurred by the time of the borrowings. It seems clear, too, from Jackson's insistence (pp. 99-100) that Brythonic was never a written language, that we are to think of all these names as having been transmitted orally from conquered to conquerors — and in their Late Brythonic or Primitive Welsh forms alone, since (p. 261) almost no one in Lowland Britain still spoke Latin. Indeed, a period of bilingualism is postulated (pp. 241-45), chiefly on the part of the Britons; while the possibility that enclaves of Britons may have survived the 'tide of conquest' in certain areas is also mooted (p. 197).

The account of the conquest put forward by Jackson in order to supply 'the necessary historical background for linguistic chronology' (p. 198) is followed by an analysis of the geographical distribution of surviving Brythonic names. Dividing England into three main Areas from east to west (Area IV consists of Cornwall together with Wales, Brythonic names in this Area being in the ascendancy), he finds that the names of Romano-British towns and of the larger rivers survive in all three; while the survival-rate of other types of name increases as one moves progressively westwards. As for the names of villages and homesteads, these are rare in Areas I and II, but common in Area III, which includes parts of Cumberland, Westmoreland, Lancashire, Shropshire, Worcestershire, Herefordshire and Gloucestershire, plus the whole of the south-west as far as the Tamar; this area also includes names of the improper compound type (our xf, xf'), which Jackson dates to not later than the 6th century.

These general findings agree fairly closely with those of Ekwall in his 1924 essay; more importantly, Jackson perceives a 'striking correlation between the frequency of Brittonic versus English names and the periods of the conquest' (p. 221). Neither Ekwall nor Jackson subscribes to the theory of extermination; at the same time, however, Ekwall (1924) thinks that it may come 'near the truth' in parts of the east — e.g. Essex, Suffolk, Norfolk — while Jackson (pp. 234-35) likewise thinks it possible that, in Area I, 'many of the natives were killed and their hamlets destroyed' in what he calls 'the hurly-burly of land-grabbing'. The gradual east-west increase of Brythonic name-survivals Jackson attributes (pp. 237-41) to the numerical inferiority of the Anglo-Saxons in Areas II and III — and more notably in the latter. Here, he says (p. 237) 'the more scanty pioneers . . . did not kill off and expel the Britons to the same degree as their forefathers had done further east.'

Some Unanswered Questions

There are, then, various points of general agreement between the work of Ekwall and that of Jackson in *Language and History in Early Britain*. Nor does Jackson voice any objection to Ekwall's use in *River Names* of what we have called the extrapolative method, though he does not always agree with Ekwall's derivations. Indeed, as hinted earlier, extrapolation will continue to be necessary if the identification of Brythonic-based names in England is to be successfully carried out, regardless of what types of names are seen as the most likely candidates for scrutiny. Equally, no one working in this field would see fit to dispute the extent of the debt owed to Jackson's formidable labours.

Yet it might still be claimed that his 1953 book leaves one or two important questions hanging in the air, and an attempt is made here to pin them down — remembering that our main concern is precisely with place-names, as distinct from Late Brythonic and Primitive Welsh sound-changes seen in isolation (this, clearly, is a subject for Celtic scholars).

First, it seems obvious that if the chronology set out in Jackson's Chapter VI ('Britons and Saxons') for the Anglo-Saxon conquest is anything like accurate, then relevant conclusions drawn by him in respect of sound-change datings using place-name forms as evidence must inevitably acquire extra force. On the other hand (and this was Ekwall's basic problem) sound-changes observed in place-names can tell us little about the chronology of the conquest itself, for which virtually our sole authority is the *Anglo-Saxon Chronicle*. In short, Jackson's own datings regarding the latter as put forward in *Language and History* have to some extent to be taken on trust; and although English place-name specialists can rest content that those names which Jackson takes as Brythonic really *are* Brythonic, they cannot perhaps rest quite so content on the chronological front.

A word first about the *Anglo-Saxon Chronicle*. Here, as we have seen, each annal is dated according to the *anno domini*, or Dionysiac, system with which we are familiar today. This, however, is misleading, since the system (devised by the monk Dionysius Exiguus in 525) was probably not introduced into England until the 7th century; the *Chronicle* sources — verse-traditions, king-lists, retrospective notes added by clerics to tables used for computing Easter — would therefore have been adapted to fit it subsequently, with varying degrees of discrepancy. Moreover, the *Chronicle* itself was not compiled until around 890, in the reign of Alfred; and although some of the material is based on Bede's *Ecclesiastical History* (c. 730), not a great deal is known about Bede's own sources for the pagan period of English history, nor about the method used by him in fixing dates for this particular period. There are internal discrepancies, too, in the *Chronicle*'s account of certain events associated with the early stages of the settlement.

If the assumption is that there was no writing among the pagan Anglo-Saxons before the beginning of the conversion in 597, this means that nearly 150 years would have passed since the date given by Bede for the first coming of these pagans (and it must be remembered that the date itself is suspect, not least for the reasons mentioned in the last paragraph). Pursuing the assumption further, we should surely be justified in thinking that writing could not have become anything like widespread before another 30 or 40 years had passed; so that on this reckoning, the written recording of place-names by Anglo-Saxon hands could scarcely have begun until the first quarter of the 7th century.

In practice, almost no place-name records are known in Old English from this sort of early date — which, of course, is only *comparatively* early. Yet even if they existed in abundance, many such records would still concern names taken over by oral transmission at varying times during a period now extending over some 175 years — or getting on for three life-spans. Even allowing for the undoubted strength of oral tradition in the two cultures concerned, one is bound to wonder how closely these (putative) records would echo names originally passed on simply by word of mouth. And further questions arise as to who, exactly, was responsible for passing them on. Illiterate and ignorant British peasants? Survivors of noble British war-bands? Or counterparts of those British monks said (by Bede) to have been slain in their hundreds by Aethelfrith of Bernicia before the battle of Chester — some of whom, at least, were presumably literate? And finally, who among the pagan Anglo-Saxons was responsible for committing the names to memory? They cannot all, surely, have been trained *scopas* (bards) with photographic memories.

It seems to the present author that none of these questions has been answered with the degree of certainty needed to lend conviction to those arguments of Professor Jackson based on the evidence of Old and Middle English place-name recordings. They appear convincing only as long as the underlying doubts are thrust to the back of one's mind. For example, we have already seen that, in the annal for 552, the name that is now Salisbury is recorded in one text of the *Anglo-Saxon Chronicle* in the form *aet Searo byrg*, and that the element *Searo* is taken as representing a Primitive Welsh *Serw* (*Language and History*, p. 260, p. 602). This would fit linguistic requirements as at the mid-6th century. But we now have to recall that the relevant text of the *Chronicle* was not written down until the last decade of the 9th century: and that indeed, when the annal for 552 refers to 'the place which is called *aet Searo byrg*' ('the is genemned aet Searo byrg'), the obvious implication is that this form was current c. 890, not — necessarily — at the time to which the annal is intended to refer.

In this instance, then, there is — ostensibly — a gap of no less than 340 years or thereabouts between the time when the Anglo-Saxons reached Old Sarum and the first written record of the name. Nor are such time-lags in any way unusual — some being very much greater. Whereas with Old Sarum — i.e. modern Salisbury — we at least know the Romano-British name (*Sorviodunum*), and that the name was definitely taken over (whatever the precise date), with cases requiring extrapolation the gap between putative arrival in an area and the first written record of a given name within it may be quite extraordinarily wide.

A typical example here is the river name **Hamps** (St). This is derived by Ekwall from **Samosispā*, Primitive Welsh **hamhesp*, 'Summer-dry', i.e. dry in summer, and according to Jackson — who thinks the derivation feasible — would first have been met with by the Anglo-Saxons c. 600 (*Language and History*, p. 520). Yet the earliest written form in English sources, *Hanespe*, occurs in a charter dating from c. 1200 — giving a time-lag of six whole centuries.

Continuing the Search

These, then, are some of the factors to be borne in mind regarding chronological frameworks within which the taking over of Late Brythonic and Primitive Welsh names by the Anglo-Saxons can be accommodated. And when we look specifically at names for which no Romano-British forms are available — thus bringing into play the extrapolative method — we find that few even of those most confidently taken as having Brythonic origins boast early forms in English sources. Moreover, most, though not all, of such names occur in western areas — or at least in areas not thought to have been drastically affected by 'the first rush of the occupation' (this is the actual phrase found on p. 229 of *Language and History*, but it is echoed more or less closely elsewhere in the chapter on 'Britons and Saxons').

When these names are examined, the majority of them are seen to be either of the topographical type, e.g. **Chetwode** (Bk), *Cétwuda* 949, a tautological hybrid consisting of Primitive Welsh **cēd*, 'wood' plus Old English *wudu* (same meaning), or of the habitative type with a topographical basis, e.g. **Rossington** (YW), *Rosington* c. 1190, which is derived by Ekwall in his *Dictionary of English Place-Names* from Primitive Welsh **ros*, 'moor' with the addition of Old English *-ing-* plus *tūn*, giving the sense (for Ekwall) '*tūn* of the people on the moor'. (An alternative sense would be '*tūn* associated with the moor'.) Jackson notes this derivation (*Language and History*, p. 533), and does not repudiate it.

It is precisely these two types of name which are generally held to increase in number as one studies the map in an east-to-west direction; and doubtless they *do* increase, if one is on the look-out for them — though not only for this reason, since it is in any case likely that, as Anglo-Saxon supremacy became an accepted and irreversible fact, more names of Brythonic origin would be recorded. (Coinings using Brythonic-based words might even have become fashionable.) Intermarriage and bilingualism, not to mention the activities of literate English clerics investigating new territories, may be of some relevance here.

(The importance of the clerical class, which has already been stressed, is shown in the present context by a reference in 682 to what is now **Creechbarrow Hill**, in Somerset. A charter in Latin of this date refers to 'the hill which is called in the Brythonic language *Cructan*' — 'Hill on the Tone' — 'among us *Crycbeorh*'. This is invaluable contemporary testimony to the survival in living speech of at least one Primitive Welsh name in the area, and to the formation from its truncated form of a tautological hybrid — **cruc* plus *beorh*, 'Hill-hill'. It also indicates that the native tongue was still being spoken here in 682.)

Returning to Rossington, the spelling of c. 1190 would appear to indicate that the *-o-* in the first element was formerly long in English; if so, this probably means that the name was coined after about 600, at which time the *-o-* in **ros* itself would have been lengthened as a result of the new quantity system in Primitive

Welsh. Beyond this, there is little if any indication when the coining might have taken place; if the -o- in Rossington was always short, it could be attributed to any time after the coming of the Anglo-Saxons to the area — a few miles south-west of the Humber estuary — where the place is situated; but no date is available for this event. (Rossington is also not far from Hatfield Chase where, in 633 — so the *Anglo-Saxon Chronicle* tells us — Edwin of Northumbria was killed by Penda in alliance with the British king Cadwallon; but perhaps it would be fanciful to suggest bilingual influence here.)

The derivation of the name Rossington (the place lies towards the eastern border of Jackson's Area II as shown in *Language and History*, p. 220) prompts the crucial question: What, exactly, are the criteria to be observed in deciding whether a name in England is or is not of Brythonic origin? Granted that, if Old English words can provide a full and satisfactory explanation for any given name, we have no justification for looking further, there is more than one case where such words cannot be shown to have existed (in respect of its first element, Rossington is a case in point). In cases like these, it seems reasonable to consider whether a Brythonic-based word might fit the bill — no matter what the geographical situation of the place.

These last nine words will doubtless smack of heresy in some quarters. But let us nevertheless take a single example from eastern England and see where it leads us. In the last resort, hypotheses are there to be shot down — a truth, of course, that cuts more than one way.

Letheringham (Sf) was spelt *Ledringaham* and *Letheringaham* in 1086. Here it is likely, though not certain, that we have to deal with an original -th- becoming -d- in late Old English before the liquid, r (the reverse change, -d- > -th-, was not unknown under the same conditions). In his *Dictionary of English Place-Names*, Ekwall suggests an Old English personal name *Lēodhere* in order to explain the first element — the sense then being '*Hām* of the people of *Lēodhere*' — while acknowledging that there is no certain evidence for this name. By way of an alternative he offers an Old

English *hlēothre (from hlēothor, 'sound', 'melody'), noting that the place is on a stream; but this unevidenced word is not included in A.H. Smith's *English Place-Name Elements* (EPNS, 1956). Meanwhile Old English lether, 'leather' would presumably not qualify as a candidate; likewise lȳthre, 'wretched', 'worthless' — a semantically unsuitable word which would probably have given a form *lither in Suffolk.

In terms of Old English, then, there is no obvious solution for Letheringham; nor does Old Norse come to the rescue. On the other hand, Welsh llethr, 'slope', 'declivity' (< *lettr-) may well come into the reckoning (Letheringham is on rising ground). When the change of Brythonic -tt- > -th- took place is uncertain. Jackson (*Language and History*, p. 567) proposes a date c. 575; but, in taking note of the form Ythan-caestir found in Bede for an original *Ottōna (Romano-British Othona, i.e. the Roman fort at Bradwell-on-Sea in Essex), which clearly shows -th-, he explains this spelling by suggesting (p. 568) that the Anglo-Saxons may only have penetrated late to this fort in a 'remote' situation: that is, not until the change -tt- > -th- had already taken place in Primitive Welsh.

It is worth remarking that the name **Leather Tor** (D) is referred in *The Place-Names of Devon* (EPNS, 1931-32) to Welsh llethr, as is pointed out by G.O. Pierce in his comments on **Lether Hall** (Gla) on pp. 225-26 of *The Place-Names of Dinas Powys Hundred* (1968). Pierce notes that, if llethr correctly explains Lether Hall, an epenthetic vowel, -e-, has appeared between -th- and -r; and — with the same proviso concerning correctness — a similar vowel may be observed in the 1086 form Letheringaham, though this would probably be an English development. (It is assumed here that Welsh llethr stems from *lettr-; but perhaps the source is *letr-, with -tr- > -thr in Welsh.)

The single example of Letheringham is offered up here as — if necessary — a sacrifice. But when we remember that little if anything is known about the Anglo-Saxon settlement of Suffolk (the *Anglo-Saxon Chronicle* does not mention it), and that nothing whatsoever is known about the fate of the British inhabitants there, it would seem that to rule out a Brythonic origin for this name on anything other than phonological grounds would involve begging more than one question. Perhaps at the very least we could think in terms of British enclaves in this ancient territory of the Trinovantes; and there is nothing inherently implausible about a hybrid name signifying '*Hām* of the people on the slope'.

(Nb: For further discussion of the name *Othona*, see *The Place-Names of Roman Britain*, by A.L.F. Rivet and Colin Smith, 1981, pp. 434-35.)

Written Sources

Attention has already been drawn to the lateness of place-name recordings in Old and Middle English when set beside the dates traditionally assigned to the first Anglo-Saxon settlements (c. 450-c. 500), the dates themselves being chiefly dependent on the authority of Bede and the *Anglo-Saxon Chronicle*. The question centred on the reliability or otherwise of place-name forms assumed to have been written down in no case earlier than 597 and in most cases long afterwards — making due allowance for the gradual spread of a literate class during the 7th century, following the Rome-based conversion. The question is no trifling one, and it seems necessary as well as fitting to conclude this book with a few thoughts concerning the possibility that some form of writing was practised throughout the whole settlement period — whether this is taken as beginning c. 450 or (as the author believes) in the 420s. Any such writing would not necessarily lessen the dating problem, but it might have significant bearing on the forms of certain names.

As regards Brythonic, Professor Jackson (*Language and History*, pp. 99-101) is adamant that this language was not written; for the Romano-British period, he effectively sees all writing in terms of Latin. But there is a degree of misplaced emphasis here. For while Jackson may well be right in arguing that Brythonic was not written for literary or administrative purposes etc., the act of writing is ultimately about the representation of the sounds of a language by a certain set of signs, or letters — not about what those letters happen to be or the particular uses to which the language in question is put.

On this view, which is surely the correct one, the very appearance of Brythonic names — called rather dismissively by Jackson (p. 100, n. 1) 'an irreducible minimum' — on coins from before the Romano-British period, as well as in Roman documents like the *Antonine Itinerary* and in a mass of later inscriptions (all of which Jackson notes, of course) amounts in itself to sufficient proof that the Brythonic language *was* written. The fact that the letters used were Roman is, in the last resort, scarcely relevant. What matters is that the alphabetic principle (one sound, one letter) had demonstrably been mastered by those who wrote or inscribed the names.

The practice of the Gauls in Caesar's time may be offered as a reasonably close parallel. In his *Gallic War* (I, 29), Caesar speaks of 'documents' (*tabulae*) found in a Helvetian camp amounting to a detailed register (*nominatim ratio*) concerning the Helvetian population — but drawn up 'in Greek letters' (*litteris Graecis*). And again (at VI, 14), we are told that the Druids of Gaul wrote down nothing connected with their doctrines, but used Greek letters for 'almost everything else' (*reliquis fere rebus*). Whatever the precise nature of this Druidic writing, it would seem to confirm the view that the particular set of signs (or alphabet) used to represent the sounds of a language is to some extent a matter of choice.*

The author is not presuming to dispute Jackson's overall argument to the effect that Latin was *the* written language in Roman Britain. What, rather, is being stressed is that it was evidently not impossible for certain types of Brythonic words to be written down or inscribed if, and when, circumstances were deemed appropriate. The information conveyed by names, both of persons and places, may indeed be an 'irreducible minimum'; but since much of Jackson's own book is concerned with precisely this

* For an overall treatment of this subject, see G.R. Driver, *Semitic Writing — From Pictograph to Alphabet*, London/Oxford, 1976.

type of information, it seems a little strange that his attitude towards it should come over as so ambivalent.

The Celtic Church

In any discussion of Brythonic and/or Romano-British place-names, the rôle of the Celtic Church must inevitably be taken into account. For all the setbacks of the 5th century, there were men of stature and sophistication among British Christians before, during and after this period. (Pelagius himself, for example, for all his heretical leanings, was both well-read and much-travelled.) And while we cannot be sure as to exactly what sources of information were available to them, British monks, taken as a class, seem the most likely people to have preserved traditions regarding place-names and — voluntarily or otherwise — to have passed them on to the Anglo-Saxons.

What we can only call 'ecclesiastical tradition' may, in fact, have specific bearing on certain names found in Bede's *History*. These names include (1) *Calcaria* (Tadcaster, YW), (2) *Campodono* (unidentified, perhaps a Roman fort at Leeds), (3) *Cataractam/Cataractone* (Catterick, YN), (4) *Dorubrevi* (Rochester, K), (5) *Doruvernis* (Canterbury, K), (6) *Lugubalia* (Carlisle, Cu), (7) *Sabrina* (the Severn), (8) *Venta* (Winchester, Ha). All these names are found in one or other of the official or semi-official Roman records (e.g. *Antonine Itinerary*) already mentioned, while *Sabrina* is also found in Tacitus (unread by Bede); but there is no *other* record of them. The question is, then, how did Bede come to know the Romano-British forms? (It should be remembered that Bede was no friend of the British Church as a whole, not least on account of the 'taint' of Pelagianism, and would be unlikely openly to acknowledge any help he might have received from that direction.)

Now as we have seen, the whole thrust of Jackson's argument in *Language and History* as regards the taking over of Brythonic-based names by the Anglo-Saxons is that it depended on oral transmission; that is, the earliest Old English forms of these names represent the stage of development they had reached in speech by the time of takeover. As we have also seen, there is more than one reason that entitles us to feel uneasy about this line of argument. Manifestly, however, the possible existence of undiscovered (and perhaps undiscoverable) written records — even of the simplest kind — adds a different dimension to the whole question. For written records might mean that, in some cases at least, Old English forms of borrowed names represent traditional or fossilised versions, not contemporary ones. (As shown by English Naunton in a later age, it is by no means unknown for an earlier form to supplant a later one *in speech*.) And while it is true that the existence of such records cannot be proved, the eight names of Bede cited above are enough to give pause for thought.

If traditional or archaic versions of names *were* passed on from Britons to Anglo-Saxons, how could we detect this? And are there any names which might be thought particularly likely to fall into this category? The first question is closely tied to the second, as will be seen by a consideration of the river name **Tamar** (D).

This was first recorded c. 150 by Ptolemy as *Tamáros*, and the medial -*m*- has persisted in all written records (as well as in speech) until the present day. Now the *Chronicle* is not specific as to when the Anglo-Saxons reached the Tamar by land, though a date in the first quarter of the 8th century seems likely; at any rate, it will have been *at least* two centuries after the time when in Late Brythonic speech, the lenition of -*m*- would have begun. (It should be noted that the name Devon, from **Dumnonii*, appears as *Defnas* in the *Chronicle* annal for 823, with -*m*-sound substituted by -*f*- in Old English, showing lenition as having occurred.) Does this apparent anomaly justify us in taking Tamar as an example of a name passed on to the Anglo-Saxons in an archaic form, written or spoken (or both), which was subsequently preserved?

In fact Tamar is only one of many Brythonic-based names containing internal -*m*- whose Old English forms also show -*m*-. In explaining this, Jackson (*Language and History*, pp. 482-94) argues that lenition of -*m*- occupied a very long period, involving two stages of 'strong' and 'weak' nasalisation before the final voiced end-product was denasalised altogether. During the whole of the 7th century, he concludes (p. 491), the Anglo-Saxons were always likely to represent lenited -*m*- either by their own -*m*- or by their -*f*- (= -*v*-). But he does (pp. 491-92) recognise that certain personal and place-names represented by -*m*- in Old English — including Tamar — constitute 'apparent contradictions'.

Jackson's general summary (pp. 492-95) regarding the lenition of -*m*- does not really concern us here. But enough has already been said to show once again the uncertainties surrounding place-name forms recorded in England when used as evidence for (or against) sound-changes in Late Brythonic and Primitive Welsh. Perhaps Jackson is right about the name Tamar; on the other hand, perhaps he is wrong. One might have assumed, for instance, that Tamar would have had time to develop to *Tavar* among the Britons of Cornwall themselves before English language and influence began to take real hold in the region as a whole — not, probably, before c. 931, when Athelstan founded a see at St Germans (with a bishop of British name, no less). Meanwhile there is no proof that the name Tamar was not already known, with -*m*- fully unlenited, to Anglo-Saxon pirates before the settlement had even started, just as there is no proof that it was not passed on later in archaic, or fossilised, form to settlers reaching the river by land. In the last resort, we simply do not know.

Runic Writing

It will be understood that previous references to 'literacy' and a 'literate class' belong in the context of a monkish secretariat using (mostly) the Latin language and the Roman alphabet, and that these people could not have been numerous in Anglo-Saxon (as distinct from British) society until about the first quarter of the 7th century. Before this sort of date, and in this sort of context, the heathen English may be considered illiterate. However, they were by no means illiterate in the broader sense, having brought with them their own fully-fledged alphabet of 24 basic characters, or runes.

The use of this alphabet was doubtless the preserve of a small specialist minority; and as was perhaps only natural, the practice of their craft gradually acquired overtones of mystery and magic. Natural, but also a pity; for these overtones have tended to linger, and serve only to mask the cold fact that runes were an integral feature of Anglo-Saxon culture — exactly how important a feature, the scarcity of the evidence makes it difficult to decide.

Probably no one today would wish to go as far as E.A. Freeman, who — in the 1879 article on early English history cited earlier — states boldly that they (the Anglo-Saxons) 'had their runic alphabet; and it is perfectly possible that the entries in the Chronicles may have come from an absolutely contemporary record.' Even if this possibility were admitted, the problem as to how any such record was fitted later into the *anno domini* system of dating would still remain. Yet something at least must be conceded to Freeman's line of reasoning. No matter how limited its nature, recording by the Anglo-Saxons from the 5th century *was* possible, since the necessary apparatus existed; whether it actually took place, or whether it involved place-names as an 'irreducible minimum', is a different question again.

In a paper published more than a century after Freeman's time ('Runic Literacy Among the Anglo-Saxons', in *Britain 400-600: Language and History*, 1990, pp. 400-401) René Derolez estimates that the runic inscriptions so far found in England may amount to no more than one per cent of the total output during the first five centuries after the Anglo-Saxon settlement. This article by Derolez has nothing to do with place-names as such, nor does he in any way suggest that place-names in runic form might be included among the inscriptions presumed lost. But one never knows what spade or bulldozer is likely to turn up. A single piece of metal, found ideally near somewhere like Salisbury, inscribed with the words *Aet Searwe* in legible runes, and with a manufacture-date c. 550-600, might do wonders for our perceptions regarding the early forms of names in England. Failing such adventitious aids, we have no choice but to go on paying lip-service to the effectiveness of oral tradition.

Select Bibliography

Alcock, Leslie, *Arthur's Britain* (London, 1989).

Bammesberger, A. and Wollmann, A. (ed.), *Britain 400-600: Language and History* (Heidelberg, 1990).

Bromwich, Rachel and Jones, R. Brinley (ed.), *Astudiaethau ar yr Hengerdd* (Caerdydd, 1978).

Davies, Wendy, *Wales in the Early Middle Ages* (Leicester, 1982).

Dexter, T.F.G., *Cornish Names* (London, 1926).

Driver, G.R., *Semitic Writing: From Pictograph to Alphabet* (London, 1976).

Evans, D. Simon, *A Grammar of Middle Welsh* (Dublin, 1970).

Foster, John, *Accent and Quantity* (London, 1820).

Frere, Sheppard, *Britannia* (London, 1978).

Gelling, Margaret, *Signposts to the Past* (London, 1988).

Jackson, Kenneth, *Language and History in Early Britain* (Edinburgh, 1953).

Jones, Bedwyr Lewis, *Enwau* (Gwasg Carreg Gwalch, 1991).

Jones, J. Morris, *A Welsh Grammar* (Oxford, 1913).

Padel, O.J., *Cornish Place-Name Elements* (Nottingham, 1985).

Padel, O.J., *A Popular Dictionary of Cornish Place-Names* (Penzance, 1988).

Pierce, Gwynedd O., *The Place-Names of Dinas Powys Hundred* (Cardiff, 1968).

Rivet, A.L.F. and Smith, Colin, *The Place-Names of Roman Britain* (London, 1981).

Smith, A.H., *English Place-Name Elements* (Cambridge, 1956).

Taylor, Isaac, *Words and Places* (London, 1864).

Thorpe, Lewis (trans.), Gerald of Wales, *The Journey Through Wales/The Description of Wales* (London, 1978).

Trépos, Pierre, *Grammaire Bretonne* (Rennes, 1980).

Walker, David, *Medieval Wales* (Cambridge, 1991).

Williams, Ifor, *Enwau Lleoedd* (Liverpool, 1962).

Wright, J. and Wright, E.M., *Old English Grammar* (Oxford, 1925).

Wright, J. and Wright, E.M., *Middle English Grammar* (Oxford, 1928).

Index